THE
RETAIL
HANDBOOK

Master **omnichannel** best practice to attract, engage
and retain customers in the **digital age**

ANTONY WELFARE

Praise

There is a good combination of strategy and 'nitty-gritty', with numerous common-sense tips based on insights from Antony's retail experience. Both the planning and the execution are well covered and each section has a helpful checklist of subjects to consider. The book is possibly unique in providing such a comprehensive practical guide to retailing in one compact volume.

Roger Best,
Chairman and former CEO of Radley

Retail has been around as long as man himself, yet I'm sure it has never before been captured in such simple prose and so comprehensively. Using real life case studies this book will offer you advice to improve your retail skills.

Mark Buckley,
Finance Director, Rapha Racing

Retail is more than just the product: it's the customer, the store colleagues, the service and the relationship between all of them. This book neatly pulls these elements together in a way that both the novice and the expert will find useful and accessible.

Neil Symons,
Head of HR Transformation Rollout,
International FTSE 100 Retailer

RETHINK PRESS

Second Edition published in Great Britain 2018
by Rethink Press (www.rethinkpress.com)

First published by Ecademy Press 2011
© Copyright Antony Welfare

CONTENTS

Foreword   9

Preface   11

Introduction   13

PART ONE: RETAIL THEN AND NOW   17

In The Beginning   19

Has Retailing Really Changed?   33

Principles Of Retailing   39

PART TWO: OMNICHANNEL RETAILING   53

The Journey From One To Omni   55

Direct-To-Consumer Retailing   67

Omnichannel Performance Indicators   77

Digital Marketing Channels   83

Content And Keywords Are Key To Success   93

Social Media   99

PART THREE: RETAIL PRINCIPLES   103

The Retail Standards   105

Know Your Customer   111

Know Your Product   127

Establish Your Brand And Niche   139

Build A Team To Compete   149

Market Your Product And Brand   161

Launch The Business And Sell, Sell, Sell   171

Customer Service Is Everything   181

Merchandise And Manage Your Stock   189

Manage Your Information And Finance   205

Build A Strong Foundation For Growth   219

Etail And Social Media Case Study   225

Acknowledgements   245

About The Author   247

For everybody living in
our digital world.

Foreword

Sam Walton, the founder of the largest retail organisation in the world, said in his autobiography *Made in America*, 'I had to get up every day with my mind set on improving something'. You may not be aiming to create another Walmart, but any independent retailer starting out or looking to improve will find *The Retail Handbook*' a very useful guide on how to do it. The book takes the reader on a well-constructed journey through the key areas that need to be considered.

There is a good combination of strategy and 'nitty-gritty', with numerous common-sense tips based on insights from Antony's retail experience. Both the planning and the execution are well covered, and each section has a helpful checklist of subjects to consider. The book is possibly unique in providing such a comprehensive practical guide to retailing in one compact volume.

Like any good business guide, the customer is always at the centre of things and I like the importance placed on values. The journey starts by challenging you to 'know your customer' and moves logically through the key functional areas of the business. There are strong sections offering up-to-date tips covering online marketing and social media.

Antony has set out to apply what he learned from his hands-on experience at large retailers such as Sainsbury, M&S and Dixons, to retail businesses of all sizes. The beauty of the book is that it offers the retailer the opportunity to exploit thinking and techniques often considered the preserve of big retail chains.

The history of Antony's retail family from the 1920s is a fascinating read and the way Antony links the old retailing skills with the current digital world shows that Retail is still Retail.

Antony shows he is passionate about his subject and this is why *The Retail Handbook* should prove relevant, positive and uplifting to any retailer and brand.

Roger Best

Retailer with over 30 years' experience leading consumer brands, and former CEO of Radley

Preface

I have the good fortune to have been born into a retailing family, and have been working in shops since the age of 15. I started work in our local newsagent after spending my younger years talking about 'the shop' with my family.

'The shop' comprised a high-street building with a ground floor shop, a warehouse and a couple of floors of living space. My great-grandfather bought the shop at 23 years old, with a mortgage, to look after his family. At the time he said to his wife, 'If we own a grocery shop we will never go hungry.' What a wise man he was.

This was back in 1923, and he opened the store with one advert in the local paper. The shop was a provisions shop – a fairly new concept in Victorian Britain. In later chapters, I will talk about life in the early days of retail and look at my extensive retail and ecommerce experience over the last few years, which has shaped this book and my retail life.

This book builds on the basics of retailing and sets out a very simple formula for retail success. Whether you are new to retailing, launching your first ecommerce business, or a multinational consumer brand looking to sell direct to the consumer, you will be able to follow my tried and tested formula for success.

Many consumer brands are looking to sell directly to their customers and this is changing the world of retail. As I discuss in the first chapter, understanding your customer is key to long-term success, and this area is one where consumer brands unequivocally lead the world. If you are a consumer brand looking to go direct or a retailer looking to grow your online business, this book is an invaluable background for your strategies and plans to be built upon.

In the book, I concentrate on the basics (something most retailers and consumer brands forget or get wrong). Getting the basics right allows you to grow and develop your retail world, both online and offline

I hope you enjoy the book, and I wish you every success with your new journey to achieving retail success.

Antony Welfare

Introduction

Welcome to *The Retail Handbook,* second edition.

The first edition was written in 2010 and was designed to help smaller retailers build a successful retail business. In the book, I covered the growth of digital technologies and the internet. I also added a case study of the first internet business I built and launched online.

Now, eight years later, I am updating the book with two key new areas of expertise. The first is to bring to the public, by way of context, real-life details of how a retail shop was developed and run in the 1920s.

The details I share in this book are from the real-life experiences of my great-grandfather and my gran in running the shop. Both worked in the shop for a number of years and over the last few years I have been working with my gran to understand how it operated back then.

The reason I include this new section is to show you that the original principles of retailing are still very relevant in today's digital world; we just apply them in a different way. I will go into details about these and will show you how to use these for your business to help you retail better, both online and offline.

The other new addition to the second edition is the inclusion of my last few years' experience in digital transformation, where I have been launching ecommerce websites and helping develop 'omnichannel' brands and global retailers.

This area follows the 'customer-first' theme and I look at the customer journey and how that has changed considerably in the last few years. We are now able to shop 24 hours a day, on any device and buy products from anywhere around the world. This poses big challenges to retailers and consumer brands. I will cover what these challenges are and how you can improve them to trade better.

This handbook is designed to take you, as a retailer, consumer brand or aspiring retailer, on a journey to understand how to run a retail business successfully. It is aimed at all retailers wishing to learn best practice from large and small retailers with whom I have worked over time.

Part One: I look back at the principles of retailing over the last century using real-life experience from the 1920s together with real-life experience from now, to give you a formula for retail success in the digital age.

The principles of retailing have not changed over time, the methods of deployment have – what are those changes and how can you benefit from understanding these in your omnichannel journey?

Part Two: I discuss 'omnichannel' and 'etail': these are very important for all retailers and consumer brands, and I have specialised in these areas for the last seven years.

Etail is the word I use to capture all things that are retail, but not using the traditional physical stores. Etail embraces the internet and uses all the power of the internet, now and in the future. It also covers new technologies such as smartphones, tablets and mobile commerce. Anything that is not a retail store, catalogue or call centre is very likely to be part of etail.

Omnichannel is when you have many channels that act as one for your customers. This is a step on from one channel to multiple channels and looks at all channels as one and inter-changeable as customers shop and research across all your sales channels.

I also introduce the all-important Customer Interaction Model. As retailing has become more complex, with online and offline interactions, understanding all your customer interactions also becomes more complex – and critical for retailing success in a digital world.

The potential of all retailers and consumer brands can be significantly enhanced with omnichannel strategies, and your time spent reading and understanding this section will pay you back with increased sales and customer satisfaction.

Part Three: I cover the main stages of your retail journey, starting with my basic retail principles.

At the heart of the book is the customer, so knowing your customer is the subject of the first chapter in this part. The subsequent chapters set out the steps to take to become a successful retailer online and offline.

1. Know your customer
2. Know your product
3. Establish your brand and niche
4. Build a team to compete
5. Market your product and brand
6. Launch the business and sell
7. Customer service

8. Merchandise and manage your stock

9. Manage your information and

10. Build a strong foundation for growth

The retail world is a challenge, but there are many things you can do to help improve your retail business. If you follow this journey, you will see significant improvements in your retail fortunes.

Part One

RETAIL THEN AND NOW

Chapter 1

In The Beginning

In Part One of the book, I will give you a real understanding of the principles and retailing best practice from four generations of retailers. I will start by talking about how modern retailing began in the 1920s and then link this through to my life today as a modern digital retailer.

I am in a very privileged position, being the fourth generation of a retailing family, and from this history I am able to share the real-life story of retailing in the 1920s. I have gained this insight over the last few years from my family history and my dear Gran, who has helped me with this part of the book.

This section is not a backward-looking history section. In this part I will tell you *how* we retailed in the past and *why* this is relevant in the digital world we live in.

Retailing basics and principles have not changed; only the way we retail has changed.

Shopping from the Victorian era onwards

Shopping and retailing was highly regulated in the past (more so than today), and it was very customer-focused on a physical basis, i.e. a physical shop which you had to go to, to buy your products. Due to regulations and the culture at the time, there was a 'one-to-one' interaction with each shop. The shop owner and staff often knew the customers and this meant a highly personalised service.

Retailing has progressed significantly over the last twenty years, but I want to quickly begin with the history of retail, starting from the Victorian era of 1837 to 1900.

This era saw the creation of the high street as we know it today. As more people moved into the towns and cities, fewer were able to grow their own produce and began to rely on shops for food and other goods. Meat and vegetables were displayed for all to see outside the shops, so the early high street looked more like what we would now call a market. The buildings had small windows to help keep the contents cool and some would have had workrooms for making the products on sale.

In the Edwardian era, from 1901 to 1914, shopping became a pastime in itself. Global shipping and cheaper imported products meant that even the poorest people were able to afford meat on occasion, and canned goods became more popular.

Department stores were also opening, such as Selfridges in 1909, bringing luxury to people as never before. Unfortunately, the start of the First World War in 1914 shattered the comforts of the early 1900s and food prices soared. This led to a different retailing world, where countries were more focused on survival than shopping as a pastime.

During the 1920s and 1930s, shop owners began to use the power of advertising and window displays to draw in customers. Goods inside were displayed in glass cabinets, and brands appeared that we would still recognise today.

Shops like Woolworths, Burtons and Boots began to dominate the UK retail market, and food became relatively cheap, with fruit and vegetables, year-round staples and tinned foods growing in popularity.

Refrigerators began to make an appearance in some domestic kitchens, allowing people to store food for longer and shop less frequently. This trend became more pronounced in later decades.

High streets started to grow and people began to shop as a pastime again. It was during this period that my family's retail world began.

The family shop

Let me introduce you to our family shop, which opened on 26 March 1923 on Sidcup High Street in Kent, England. The shop was opened by my great-grandfather, H.H. Chapman – known as Jack.

He bought the shop as a grocer's shop, with an attached warehouse for the distribution of goods from wholesalers to other local outlets. He was a bacon expert and his swinging sign was 'The Bacon Specialist'.

His wife, Rose, worked on the cash desk, where they had the first 'automated' system of little metal containers going along a wire to the counters.

There was a large bike with a nameplate on the crossbar for the errand boy and there were two counter hands -a male for the bacon and wet goods, and a female for the dry goods.

THE RETAILER H.H. CHAPMAN

Jack was a man ahead of his time in many ways. He had many ideas, thrived on hard work and would do anything he could for anyone in need. He was very well-liked in the town, not least at the Sidcup & District Recreational Club, where he eventually became their President for the duration of the Second World War.

He had a definite flair for business from an early age and was determined not to be just a small corner shop owner. When he bought the high street shop, it was mortgaged to the hilt, but as he said, 'At least we won't starve in a grocer's shop!'

He had plans for the warehouse, and he soon became the local distributor for many commodities from Peak Frean, Nestle, Walls and many more, which was additional income.

He never refused a special request from his pampered clients, even if it meant obtaining an item from London (some 15 miles away), and he always delivered after hours if necessary. They also had to deliver plain brown envelopes, which meant an account was outstanding. Consumer credit was given in those days on a personal basis as there were no bank and credit reports.

He obtained the latest equipment and was the first to have an electric bacon/ham slicer, although he was a skilled man and could cut a slice paper-thin with his carving knives, sharpened by a steel sharpener.

His two front window displays of the double-fronted shop were legendary and members of staff were often made to go in between them to tidy up or dust.

There was a large tradesman's bike with the logo 'H. Chapman - the Bacon Specialist' painted under the cross-bar and an errand boy to ride it. The same logo was also on a swinging sign outside the shop. This was his pride and joy and a very important marketing message for customers walking down the high street. They definitely knew where to buy bacon.

He won several Chamber of Trade awards, was a Fellow of the Grocers' Institute and at one time the President.

How the shop operated

This was the only privately-owned grocery shop on the high street when Jack bought it, and probably for many years after. The others, Liptons and Cave Austin (which also ran an off-licence), were company-owned.

In those days (1920s and 1930s), grocers were not licensed to sell meat, fish, milk, bakery goods or fruit and vegetables, and this was strictly adhered to. It could take some time to buy the family shopping from different outlets, but there was not always a desire to go into town for weekly shopping trips. Although the choices would have been greater there and possibly cheaper, not everyone had cars and it was difficult to travel with full baskets on the buses.

At the time on Sidcup High Street there were: a large toy/ hobby shop, ladies and gents' outfitters, 50 Shilling Tailors, Express Dairies, Dolcis Shoes, Boots the Chemists, four major banks, a police station at the far end, and a bus stop next to the Black Horse public house/restaurant, both of which were conveniently opposite the shop.

Bacon was purchased direct from Denmark and stored in the warehouse until required. The cutting up was a good half day's work, usually done on Thursday afternoons (half day closing).

Jack wore starched white coats (like a doctor) and starched aprons that tied around and in front, until soiled, and then he used fresh ones. The laundry van came twice a week to facilitate this. He wore a straw boater in the summer, as did many tradesmen then, and a panama hat at weekends.

The shop layout

The interior was well set out: the left side was a glass topped and fronted large counter for display, with working space behind on which was the large electric slicing machine (the very latest design in 1923).

There were cheeses (to be cut by wires), butter and lard to be weighed out, with bacon to be sliced according to the thickness desired by the customer, and home cooked ham, also to be sliced. Butter was kept in wooden churns and scooped out with wooden spatulas, patted into blocks on greaseproof paper and weighed.

The ham was cooked in the small kitchen by his wife, in big iron pots. It was skinned with some white fat left on (for flavour) and then dusted with fine breadcrumbs and displayed on white pottery stands. There were also some sausages and ready-baked pork pies; small ones and larger ones with hardboiled egg inserts to be sliced. Everything was done by hand in the shop.

On the far end of the left side was shelving to the ceiling that housed dry goods – sugar, rice, tea, dried fruit, etc. – which were also scooped out, weighed and poured into strong blue bags.

The front of the wooden counter displayed tins of biscuits – all as weigh out, no pre-packed in those days – and there were few varieties: rich tea, gingers, custard creams, digestives and garibaldi. Any broken ones were sold as a mixture at half-price.

The cash desk was at the far end on a raised platform and was enclosed in glass, where Jack's wife, Rose, reigned supreme over the metal contraptions from both counters that sent little containers along a wire with an invoice and cash. Rose then sent back the stamped receipt and change back to customers. She was quite statuesque, dark-haired and quietly spoken, and wore a navy blue suit or dress with a white collar.

If the customer had an account to pay weekly or monthly or even quarterly, the invoices remained in the book at the respective counters.

Under and in front of the cash desk were 'special offers' of the day, and past the door to the interior were shelves with cereal packets and tinned goods, which the staff removed at the customer's request. Further along was a glass case housing Lyons cakes, the only bakery items allowed for sale in a grocer's shop. These included Swiss rolls, jam tarts, Victoria sponge cakes, 'French cream' sandwiches and the speciality frosted coconut 'snow' cakes.

At the end, in front of the window, was a table with flowers for sale and two or three chairs for the customers to sit on while waiting to be served or to have their purchases packed up. They could be delivered later in the day if required, for a small charge, by the boy with a tradesman's bike, basket in front and carrier behind.

Orders were made up as soon possible and any not ready by close had to be finished first thing the next morning. Jack would help each lady across to the chair in front of his counter as if she were the only one there (good salesmanship). Many of them lived in large comfortable houses (mini stately homes) with probably a minimum of three servants: parlour maid, cook and gardener. They often required items for dinner parties and if something was not readily available, Jack would 'phone a place in London' and get it out on the next train down. He would then deliver it as late as 10 p.m.

From time to time, if their accounts had not been paid, his daughters were sent after school on the bike to deliver a plain brown envelope to the lady of the house, who greeted them cordially… until she saw what they were delivering!

The shop was open five and a half days a week: Monday to Wednesday, from 8.30 a.m. to 6 p.m.; Friday and Saturday, from 8.30 a.m. to 9 p.m.; and half day on Thursday, closing at 12.30 p.m. Lunch hour was from 12.30 p.m. to 2 p.m., strictly enforced, to tidy up, sweep the floor and replenish stocks. The maid from upstairs would help with this. Deliveries were made, as and when required, in brown carrier bags and surplus empty boxes.

Market garden centre

JACK AND ROSE CHAPMAN AT SIDCUP NURSERIES

During the early 1930s, Jack loaned one thousand pounds to a friend whose business was in a bad way, but unfortunately the poor man committed suicide because of his situation. His solicitor advised that Jack take as repayment a small market garden, valued at that amount, instead of waiting as a creditor. Jack took on The Limes Nursery on Sidcup Hill, which was somewhat of a challenge, but he was always 'up for a gamble'.

He knew nothing about growing, but the foreman, Frank, went with the deal and they had a great working relationship over the years. So much so, that Jack built the largest greenhouses in Kent - from some he had seen in Holland - that were two storeys high and his pride and joy. Tomatoes were his speciality, and he grew lettuce, cucumbers, and spring onions, and had a mushroom house. Flowers were daffodils, and then sweet peas in the summer - six houses, all of a different colour, mostly packed and sent by train to London markets and the big hotels. He also had a field of tulips, later gladioli.

In the autumn there were chrysanthemums in open plots and various pot plants for Christmas sale. The houses were heated by hot water pipes and when a frost occurred it was all hands on deck to start the boilers using wood chips, small pieces of coal, twigs and then coke.

Jack also acquired several fields in St Mary Cray to grow soft fruit: strawberries, raspberries, gooseberries and red, white (rare) and black currants. It seemed as if everything he touched did well because he was a hard, dedicated worker - over at the nursery before 6 a.m., after his midday meal and not back until after 6 p.m. There was a small shop at the front of the property to sell the fresh produce, in addition to most of it going to markets.

Jack had his 'empire' and he was still not yet 40 years of age.

The nursery was badly bombed during the Second World War and the shop traded under our family ownership until the outbreak of that war, when the family sold the goodwill to a new owner. We continued to own the buildings until 2015, when we finally sold the entire business.

'The House of Quality'

As a final instalment of my history, I want to share an article about H.H. Chapman's shop that was published in *The Grocer* magazine in 1928, which I quote below. This article was written in a golden age and it is well worth reading the exact language that was used back in the 1920s.

THE HOUSE OF QUALITY

It is a proud boast which Mr. H. Chapman makes for his business. A slogan, a descriptive term which will, wherever uttered, at once bring to mind a definite place or thing has more to do with the success thereof than anything of which we know. And the beauty of such a slogan is, that its influence spreads.

We associate the term 'Quality' with a business, and for the future, whenever we hear that word, and in whatever connection we may hear it, we at once call to mind the place or person with whom we first heard it associated, and thus a subconscious advertisement is at once recalled.

It is the same with Mr. Chapman's business. He calls it 'The House of Quality and Efficient Service', and one has only to wander into the premises at 6, High Street, Sidcup, to learn how justly the term is applied, and to know that it is no vain boast.

Modernity is found in every part of it. The exterior is a modern one. The interior is even more so, since all the latest designs and proposals in regard to storage and fittings and every other appliance which may make the better, cleaner, or quicker service will be found there.

People in general are waking up to the necessity for the utmost cleanliness in regard to food stuffs. For many a long year, English people were the most careless and slovenly on earth in these matters. But the awakening has come, and the old time exposure to air, dust, dirt, contamination of all sorts, and particularly to the diseases which are carried from place to place by itinerant and

*marauding insects flies, gnats, and the like, are
all now practically things of the past.*

*The proof cases at Chapman's Stores will well
illustrate this point. Once the goods are enclosed
therein, a storm of dust might arise, without
a particle finding its way to the interior. And
this is but a single example of the care taken
to protect the goods, and, of course, the public.*

*These stores have become very popular in
Sidcup. They have gained fame by reason of
the proprietors own particular brands of bacon
and other lines, all of the highest quality, as
well as all other breakfast commodities, table
delicacies, and the like. In fact, all that one may
desire and expect to find in a good class
grocers and provision merchants, is here.*

Chapter 2

Has Retailing Really Changed?

All this nostalgia leads me on to where we are today. We are in a seriously digital world with technology, processes and products that were inconceivable in the 1920s.

The big question is: has retailing really changed since the 1920s?

My answer is... yes and no. As you can imagine, the way we retail now is significantly different, *but* the reason for retail and the success factors have not changed. Retail is still the same as it was in the 1920s. Let me show you why I believe this.

Methods of deployment

Firstly, the way we retail is very different. In the 1920s, we had a physical shop, governed and controlled by rules and regulations. We still have the shop, but we have much, much more. The customer journey is varied and complex. We have many different interaction points in the retail process - in the 1920s we had one... the physical shop!

Here is a list of some of the interaction points we have now - there are more and there are new interaction points continually appearing:

- Website
- Mobile site
- Apps
- Search engines
- Digital marketing
- TV
- Posters
- Blogs
- Social Media
- Home delivery
- Collect at store
- Radio
- Podcasts
- Games/Gamification
- Loyalty cards
- Cryptocurrency
- Blockchain Technology
- The Internet of things

What this now means for retailers is much more complexity and a more challenging process. When you had one shop and a high street there was a captive market. Now you are competing worldwide with physical and online stores open 24 hours a day.

The second big difference is our culture and the lifestyles we now lead. We have progressed through the industrial revolution and we are well into the technology e-revolution.

This has changed our retail world in many ways:

- Technology
- Speed
- Travel
- International
- Standards
- Economics

The 'E-Revolution'

I would like to introduce the 'E-Revolution' and show you how the new world we live in – and do business in – has been made possible because of major changes in technology and ecommerce.

Ecommerce businesses have used the internet and social media to change our lives forever and make our world a much more connected and technology-led environment. The speed of growth of the internet, technologies and social media, which make up the 'E-Revolution', has allowed transactions to happen online. Once transactions started happening online, the business world that we knew changed and online transactions and trading opened up a new world to all businesses.

Businesses must start to utilise the world we now live in, where 'e-transactions' are commonplace and growing.

There are different ways e-transactions are taking place; you can sell your products and services across the world; you can download digital media from around the world; and you can research information all around the world.

Not only have e-transactions changed the world, connected and mobile devices have revolutionised the way we live our lives, both personal and business. We now have access to many different connected devices – a desktop PC, mobile phone, tablet PC, laptop and other devices. For now, and the future, these mobile devices are where we can order products and services.

Your customers can download a podcast, or a PDF training guide. They can watch a video on how to do something, or they can order your physical products and get them delivered to their house or their office or the nearest train station.

The E-Revolution is allowing every business to transact mobile-wise and technically, anywhere in the world, at any time.

What are the principles of retailing that we can learn from the 1920s?

There are a number of core retail principles that make a successful retail business. Here, I look at how these principles were engaged in the 1920s and how we use them now. You will see that the principles of retail have not changed. Understanding and appreciating the past is important for success in the digital world we live in.

That said, we must adapt our mind-set and the way we retail. Old systems, processes and procedures will slow down retail growth, and larger organisations are struggling to adapt quickly enough to the new world.

My advice to CEOs and leaders in retailers and consumer brands is to start your digital transformation now. It is a journey and it will not stop, but you have to start changing now. If you do not, you will be left behind and be listed as 'out of business'. Just look at the last few years on the high street. There are many retailers that have closed because they didn't change.

Chapter 3

Principles Of Retailing

Customer first - personalisation

In the past, the retailer and their staff knew each customer personally and could offer a highly personalised experience in the shop. As travel and technology have grown, customer relationship management (CRM) has increased, making knowing an individual customer harder. Personalisation is now the key to success.

Retailers tend to use customer segmentation (later chapter) for their customer groups. This categorises all customers into certain groups and you market to those certain groups.

Customers want more: they want to be treated as a single person - exactly like customers were treated in the 1920s. This means the personalisation of CRM must progress as technology and the retailers' understanding of customers grows. Emails and social media allow retailers to understand and listen to their customers 24 hours a day across the world. This data can then be used to tailor messages and ranges to individual customers.

To offer a personalised experience, you must build your customer knowledge. Capturing data and 'big data' is an important area to focus on. If you have data on your customers, you can attempt to pre-empt their buying decisions and let them know that they need a product before they know they need it.

Amazon is pioneering this approach. They are using past purchase history, together with shopping and social data, to predict what a customer may like to buy next.

Another iteration of this is the subscription model and 'one button ordering'. These are being trialled for household products, where you can automatically have washing powder sent every month, or you press a button on your washing machine and it orders the washing powder for you.

There are many technological advances making this possible, but using and understanding your customer data is key.

Location, location, location – be everywhere

This is one of the main principles of retailing. The high street or shopping centre was key and central to the success of businesses in the past. Now, location is about being everywhere for your customers – online and offline.

We have become omnichannel and customers want what they want, when and where they want it. This means you must have a co-ordinated network of shops and be online to ensure a customer can buy what they want, where they want it. In part two of the book, I cover this in depth.

Competition – vast and global

The competition on the high street was limited and controlled by physical restrictions and governments. As shopping centres and out-of-town shopping grew, the competition increased but was still limited by physical location.

In the early 2000s, I was commercial planning manager at Marks & Spencer. Part of my role was to use customer insight data to map out areas of the country where there was no, or limited, access to an M&S store. This work looked at drive times and road networks to map the optimum stores layout. This work is now obsolete as customers can order and get a delivery from M&S anywhere in the world.

Competition is now worldwide and 24-7 – there are no borders online and customers know this. A customer can purchase items from almost any country and have those products delivered directly to their door – your competition is now global rather than local.

Once you trade online, you open yourself up to the 'one click away' or 'one swipe away' world. If a customer does not like your website, they can immediately move to your competitors' websites. For the first time they are milliseconds away from your competitors.

With more than a billion websites and billions of shops, the competition is the fiercest it has ever been. This confirms why your retailing foundations and 'customer first' thinking are key to success in a highly competitive world.

Branding must be controlled online

Establishing your brand values was important to attract people to your store, to understand what you sold and give you credibility. Your brand was represented in many physical forms, all of which were controlled by the brand and the retailer.

We are now a digital first world, where customers will see your brand online in many different places, as well as offline. Brand values dictate who you are and need to show through in every asset, online and offline.

If you take the complex customer journey, you will understand that a customer sees your brand assets* online and offline. Imagine the impact of your customers seeing your brand online shown incorrectly. This will affect their perception of your brand. Owning all your assets online and offline is a key success factor.

Retailing quality standards are key

Standards were extremely important as expectations in Victorian Britain were high. In the first chapter I shared a magazine article from 1928, which talked about the quality of our family shop and the cleanliness of the shop fittings.

Understanding quality is more difficult when you cannot touch or feel the product. Product content online (images, video, words, etc.) need to be of a high quality to ensure that the product standards are shared correctly.

Standards now relate to how you use and share your assets online. Are all your assets of the correct standard for your values? Many examples can be found online of retailers and consumer brands displaying low quality images and text

---

*   Brand assets are all the images, text, videos, sound and representation of your brand online and offline.

full of errors. A lack of attention to detail and quality enforcement will, and does, damage a brand, online and offline.

Service as an online differentiator

Offering extra services was at the discretion of the shop owner. Home delivery and credit were two common services in old retailing that helped create loyalty to the shop. A great example of extra services for our shop was the 'London requests'. This was where a good customer requested items, which we did not sell, but we knew that we could source them from London. This meant that Jack sent one of the team on a train to London to purchase the items and bring them back for the customer on that day. What a great customer experience that must have been back then.

Customers now expect a significant range of services – from home delivery and collection, and 1-hour delivery, to a finance plan. Expectations are high and service is a key online differentiator.

The costs of these services must be considered. Do your customers value all your services? Do they need all your services? Adding the right services will add value to your brand and business, but careful and targeted use of these must be the main priority.

Offering a different service to your competitors can be seen as a great loyalty driver. A great example is Amazon Prime, where you pay a yearly fee and gain free next day delivery and receive extra services such as streaming TV. This does two things for the customer: first, it ties them into you for at least a year, and second, it means that they are using your wider services and being open to your brand on a more regular basis.

Advertising and marketing have changed

Advertising was the main form of marketing in the 1920s, and was often the local newspaper. Travel was not too common, so your local high street was where to go. TV and radio were added later on, as well as magazine advertising.

Advertising is now mainly digital – in 2016, the value of digital marketing overtook the value of traditional marketing in the UK and USA, a trend that is continuing at pace. Online advertising, in all its forms, helps both online and offline sales, but consistency and targeting are still key.

Marketing is now digitally-led. After all, most of your customers will be influenced by digital marketing during their customer journey. This means that you need to be in control of your entire marketing campaign, across all your channels (online and offline). It has been proven that a fully co-ordinated advertising campaign is much more successful than separate campaigns. For example, the Christmas TV advert is a big draw in the UK for the main retailers. The best retailers develop a theme and that is used across all channels – TV, press, social media and digital marketing channels. This ensures the customer sees and 'feels' the marketing message throughout their entire customer journey.

Listings are now search engines

In the 1920s there were local listing books, which showed the address, phone number and type of shop. Over the years, this became more informative and even allowed adverts.

We now live in the world of search engines (Google, Biadu, Bing, etc.) that have made finding the information we want easy. Together with marketplaces, these form the majority of search queries for customers.

Easy search is now an accepted way of life for customers, but with ever-increasing competition and data, all retailers must ensure that the basics of their online world are correct. The main topic here is search engine optimisation or SEO. In its simplest form, good SEO means great content, which is correct, useful for the customer and of great quality.

Community

Community life was centred on the high streets and keeping your community happy was important. Understanding your community and their needs meant more business and happy customers. If you could delight your community with a range of products they wanted, you had a loyal community for your shop.

We now live in a mixed online and offline community. Online social media is growing exponentially, allowing people to communicate globally as well as locally. Using social media to help engage your community is a complex task. With many different networks and a differing usage of social media across your customer base, you need to be strategic and comprehensive with your social media strategy.

There are also many different physical communities, which make the whole omnichannel community much more complex than before. This includes the whole world of migration, which brings different communities to new areas – meaning great new opportunities for omnichannel retailers in that area.

Sourcing and the supply chain

The supply chain of any retailer and brand is critical. In the 1920s, finding a reliable source of products across the world had big challenges – there were very few flights, but the same rules applied for finding and nurturing a good supply base.

The wholesaler was much more important in the past. Part of the extension of our family shop was to build a warehouse at the back to wholesale products to other retailers in the area. We were the main wholesaler of bacon in the early 1920s and we also stocked grocery items, such as Lipton tea and Sun-Maid raisins. Not only did this give us a better price for our own stock, it meant we made a small profit selling on to other retailers in the area.

The internet and technology have allowed sourcing to become much easier and quicker. Flights are frequent and at a reasonable price, and shipping is reliable. The complexity here is now finding an exclusive set of products. This is a big challenge as it is easy to copy products worldwide.

Truly unique products rarely exist now, which takes me back to the previous principles where service has become the differentiator for retailers.

Payments and digital currency

Payments were made in either cash or 'credit' for most of the early retailing years. My family shop gave credit to 'the best customers', but this had to be paid in cash soon after.

Credit cards and contactless payments are now common. More and more electronic payments are happening, which is reducing the need for 'real cash'. This saves costs for the retailer and helps speed up transactions and customer queues.

Payments are evolving rapidly and the whole banking system is undergoing a digital transformation. New technology is being tried and tested.

Contactless cards: These are growing massively for payments without the need to use a PIN to confirm the transaction. This means a quick and convenient transaction for the customer and allows retailers to use mobile tills to save queues and frustrations in store.

Phone payments: For example, Apple Pay and Android Pay. This is where you enable your mobile phone to make payments using your cards stored on them. We are all carrying mobile phones and can use them for payments instead of cards in our wallets.

Digital wallets: These are a digital version of your physical wallet where you store your payment cards data. The benefit of this is that they also store loyalty card data. For a retailer, this is key to tracking the customer and understanding their shopping journey. Making your loyalty card available on the phone means customers are very likely to have them at the point of transaction. This allows a quick and convenient customer transaction and richer data about the customer for the retailer.

QR codes: These have been used to help link physical and digital data and experience. When a customer scans the QR code (normally on a physical product or item) they are taken to the website of the retailer. This could be used for feedback, marketing or promotional use, but it allows the retailer to track the physical and digital interaction. QR codes are widely used in China, where they have QR codes on everything. These can be used for payments, to order a taxi, to send a dating profile to a possible date, to call a person and order food - the QR code has endless possibilities, which enables many clever interactions with customers that can be measured.

Cryptocurrency: This is digital currency that has no boundary and only simple processing costs. The best known currently are Bitcoin and Ethereum and their values change daily based on demand (like a normal currency). What they offer digital retailing is a borderless payment currency - the value is the same in any country and this excites retailers as it means simplicity and clarity. Many retailers are starting to accept these currencies although take up by customers is still slow.

Blockchain technology: This could transform the banking sector and the contracts world. The foundation of a blockchain is a distributed ledger (or record) of a transaction, which is held on many computers, not just one system. This means that there is no central control of the transaction and it can be made across the world for a fraction of the cost of a current currency payment. This technology is new but growing massively and has the potential to transform payments for retailers and customers.

Principles overview

I strongly believe that learning from the past has benefits for now and for the future, and I hope I have given you an insight into retailing in the 1920s and how the principles still apply today.

RETAIL PRINCIPLES

Principle	Then	Now
Customer first	Customer relationships – the retailer and their staff knew each customer personally and could offer a highly personalised experience in the shop	Customer relationship management makes knowing a customer harder, but personalisation is key to success now.
Location, location, location	The high street was key and central to the success of the business	Location is about being everywhere for your customers – online and offline. We are now omnichannel and customers want what they want, when and where they want it
Competition	The competition on the high street was limited and also controlled	Competition is global and 24-7 – there are no borders to online and customers know this

Principle	Then	Now
Branding	Establishing your brand values was important to get people to your store	Brand values dictate who you are and need to show through in every asset online and offline
Standards	Standards were extremely important as expectations in Victorian Britain were high	Understanding standards is more difficult when you cannot touch or feel the product
Services – e.g. home delivery	Offering extra services were at the discretion of the shop owner. Home delivery and credit were two common services in old retailing	Customers now expect a significant range of services – from home delivery to collection, to 1-hour delivery, to a finance plan.
Advertising	The main form of adverting in the 1920s was the local newspaper. TV and radio were added later on, as well as magazine advertising	Advertising is now very digital – in 2016, the value of digital marketing overtook the value of traditional marketing in the UK, a trend that will continue
Listings	In the 1920s there were local listing books showing the address, phone number and type of shop	We now live in the world of search engines (Google, Biadu, Bing etc.) that have made finding what we want easy
PR	The press was the only real form of PR in the old days, with magazine and newspaper articles being the main outlets	PR now covers online and offline, with a co-ordinated campaign being the best option for the future

Principle	Then	Now
Community	Community life was centred on the high streets and keeping your community happy was very important	We now live in a mixed online and offline community. Online social media is growing exponentially, allowing people to communicate globally as well as locally
Sourcing/ Exclusives – and the supply chain	The supply chain of any retail and brand is critical. In the 1920s, finding a reliable source of products across the world had big challenges – there were few flights available	The internet has allowed sourcing to become much easier and quicker. Flights are frequent and priced reasonably and shipping is reliable
Payments	Payments were made in the form of cash or 'credit' for most of the early retailing years	Credit cards and contactless payments are now common. More electronic payment methods are being used, which is reducing the need for 'real cash'

Summary

How to maximise the learnings from the past:

- Know your customer –talking to your customer face-to-face in the past is now online and social interactions
- Tell them what you sell – 'Bacon Specialist' was the high street sign in the past. Keywords online are the new standard

- Excel in service and quality - high standards were important in the past and now customer experience and user experience is key online
- Offer extra services – home delivery from the shop using a bike is now click and collect or locker collection
- Location – the high street location is now Google, page one
- Personalisation – know your customer and target them with personalised adverts and messages

Part Two

OMNICHANNEL RETAILING

Chapter 4

The Journey From One To Omni

Retail has changed beyond recognition in the last few years and we have now seen a few years of strong growth in, and the emergence of, ecommerce – the selling of products to customers via the internet. There are many names for this: online shops, internet shops and ecommerce are the main ones.

I have been part of the 'internet revolution' from the late 1990s, when I was lucky enough to have an internet connection at my university dormitory. It was during this time that I realised that internet retailing has always been in retail: R… etail. Remove the R and you have the word 'etail' – so it has always been a part of retail, we just never noticed it.

'Etail' is extremely important, and I would now say a pre-requisite for any serious retailer. Whatever you sell and wherever you sell it you must have a website, and it should be a transactional ecommerce website.

Retail has evolved from one method of interaction and fulfilment to a global inter-related set of channels. We started the retail world with one physical shop, which was the only place you could buy the product. This kept life simple for the retailer, as they only had to look after one physical asset and market to the customers this one destination. As retail took off and retailers became more successful, they needed more shops. Retailers would open up one, two, three more shops, often in areas near the first shop. These would all be run in a similar way with the same type of stock. Often a warehouse was used to store all the stock for all the shops. This ensured a better deal for buying your stock in volume, and also a better range for customers.

We then progressed to multiple channels for retail (i.e. catalogue, online, mobile, telephone and social). This was where the physical store network was supported (but not normally connected) to new channels. The internet has become the biggest new channel, with online shops taking vast sums of money through their websites.

With these multiple channels there was little or no connection between them and so we progressed to multichannel retail. This is where you had multiple channels of operation, which were selling similar products to similar customers with some inter-relationship. For example, you could look at the website and see if the retailer sold a product you wanted and then go into store and try to find it.

This led to poor customer service, as often the product was not in store, which led us to where we are now with omnichannel retail. Omnichannel retail is looking at your customer as one through all channels – hence the word 'omni', which is Latin for 'all'.

A customer does not care about your business systems and processes, which mean that channels could be separate. If they want your product in a store or to order it on their mobile, they must be able to. The key to success here is to offer your customer what they want, need and desire when and where they want it.

Your systems must view the customer as one person, and allow them to shop online, offline and over the other channels. A great example of this is 'collect at store', where a customer orders a product online and goes in store to collect it. This should be a seamless process, and when the customer arrives, the order should be ready.

Too many retailers and brands have legacy systems that do not allow easy communication between channels, but the customer does not care about your systems issues. They want a smooth and consistent experience wherever they choose to trade with you.

The customer journey

The evolution of retail has led to a large and complex customer journey – a journey which all retailers and brands must now try to understand. Gone are the days where customers shopped in one or two physical shops (like my great-grandfather's). Customers now shop in many shops, on many devices, and with many more retailers and brands.

The customer journey has evolved and I like to view this as the customer quest and the customer interaction points. Customers can now shop in many different ways online and offline. Before they make the decision to buy, they will do research online and offline. This is a big challenge to all retailers and brands – you now need to be present in each and every interaction point; not only present, but with good quality assets and consistent messaging.

Customer interaction points are where a customer will see your brand and products on their quest and include:

- Physical stores
- Websites
- Mobile websites and apps
- TV/Radio/Billboards
- Press – Magazines/Newspapers
- Social Media
- Digital marketing

Most journeys start with an online search (a search engine such as Google or Biadu or a marketplace such as Amazon or Tmall). This will then take the customer down many different routes online and offline.

At each stage online, a retailer and brand must ensure that their assets are good quality and the messaging is consistent – imagine a customer clicking onto a website link and ending up on a page with a photograph of your product, which has been taken with a personal camera (this does happen).

Customer journey phases

A customer will still go through a structured process to buy your products and this will likely be a mix of online and offline interaction points. This will change each time, but will usually include four stages:

1. Awareness – the customer is aware that they have a want, need or desire for a product

2. Research – the customer finds out more about this product

3. Purchase – the customer buys the product

4. After-sales – the customer interacts with the retailer after the purchase

EXAMPLES OF ONLINE AND OFFLINE PHASES

Phase	Online	Offline
Awareness	Advert, social media, blog, email, video	TV advert, billboard, a friend tells them
Research	Search engines – Google, Biadu Marketplaces – Amazon, eBay	Ask friends, go into a shop
Purchase	Website, mobile app, desktop site	In store, on the phone, from a catalogue
After-sales	Emails, social media, complaints, Twitter complaints, reviews online	Go back to store, complain to friends, write a letter

The key to success for any retailer is to be present in all the interaction points and channels where your customer wants to interact with you. This may mean that some of these channels are not owned by you, but maybe run by a partner or another brand. For example, when buying a branded laptop, the customer may research the laptop on the brand website and then come to the retailer's shop and website to buy the product.

The Customer Interaction Model

At this point, I want to introduce you to my Customer Interaction Model (CIM). I have developed this model over the years to help retailers and brands understand the complexities of retailing in a digital world.

The customer in the digital age shops in a very complex way - using all your interaction points online and offline. They shop 24 hours a day and will connect with your interactions points at different times and in different ways.

In the model the customer progresses from one level to another, using physical and digital interaction points. The customer may miss a level, or may spend a long time on one level.

Customers will visit your interaction points as many times as they see fit for each product journey. This could be one or two interactions, or hundreds of interactions.

The most important learning is that each interaction point is unique to the customer at that single moment, and all the previous and future interactions points must flow and 'feel' as one.

Content is key in the interaction points - whether physical or digital. The content must reflect the brand, the product and help the customer on their journey to purchase.

STAGES OF THE CUSTOMER INTERACTION MODEL

EXAMPLES OF CUSTOMER INTERACTION POINTS

Awareness	Consideration	Conversion	Experience purchase	Advocacy
Prior purchase	Product/user reviews	Social stores	Subscription	Social media
Store presence	In-store staff	Mail order	Upsells	Reviews
Online and offline adverts	Blogs	In-store	Customer service	Gifting
Social media	Trials and testers	Partner site	Product use	Recommend a friend
Friends	Site information	Marketplaces	FAQs	Word of mouth
	Live chat	Brand site	Instructions	
		Mobile store	Returns process	
		Voice store		

At every interaction point you must ask yourself the following questions:

- Does this interaction represent my brand?
- Does this interaction help the customer onto the next interaction point?
- Is this interaction point relevant to this particular stage of the customer's interaction?
- Does this interaction point fit perfectly with the other interaction points?
- How can I improve this interaction point?

To find out more about the Customer Interaction Model please visit: www.retailpotential.com/cim

Why embrace omnichannel and move online?

Becoming an omnichannel retailer is the most important element of all current successful retailers. Omnichannel retailing is the supply of products to your customers via many different channels, with the main channels being: a physical store, a mobile-first ecommerce website and a call centre (plus new technologies and channels, which are emerging).

I cannot stress how important an ecommerce website is for retailers to grow – a true omnichannel retailer will be able to thrive and succeed in the competitive world we live in.

The online retailer case study (see Chapter 21) in this book will help you to understand the opportunities you can gain from having a good ecommerce website. Here, I discuss how we set up an internet-only retailer and the success of this business, which managed to sell our products in many countries around the world in a short space of time.

Without the internet channel, we would not have been able to sell FreshMax Shirts globally. We would also have missed the opportunity to sell our fabric and technology into existing retailers all over the world. If we had not launched and sold the shirts online in the first place, we would not have made people aware of the fabric, the shirts and the brand.

Increased ability to compete by being online

Setting up an ecommerce website will open up channels and opportunities that you would have never expected to be available to your business as a physical retailer only. The internet is 24/7 and available across the world. The potential market for your business, product and brand is truly global – there are no borders to the internet (apart from a few restricted countries).

You will be able to reach a wider local market, i.e. more people in your town, district, and even country, as well as a wider world market. This potential gives you the opportunity to grow your business in ways that you had never dreamed of growing it.

More customers will see your brand and your products, giving you a wider customer base on which you can sell more products and make more customers happy.

You must be omnichannel in your vision for your ecommerce channel. This means that you must view your physical stores and your website in exactly the same way – they are two different 'routes' to the same business. They sell the same products, to the same customer segment, in the same way – the only difference is the medium the customer uses to interact with your business and the delivery methods.

How an omnichannel approach helps you compete:

- Allows a world-wide market potential for your products and brand
- Allows your channels to cross sell and integrate with each other
- Opens up markets and customer segments you never thought you could reach
- Allows you to grow your business and therefore get better buying prices and be more competitive than your competitors

- Allows you to disseminate much more information to your customers about your brand and products
- Enables the customers to interact with your brand – to understand the stories behind the business and engage in discussion with your business
- Give you the ability to grow your product range
- Gives you new marketing channels both online and offline

Summary

For many retailers the journey to omnichannel retail is now well established. Customers now demand their products where and when they want them, and retailers in general have adapted to this challenge.

The complexity of omnichannel means that retailers and brands struggle to keep all their interactions consistent and of good quality. With a significantly wider channel base, keeping up with customer interactions is key. The CIM shows customers' complex buying requirements, and retailers must improve on all the interaction points.

Chapter 5

Direct-To-Consumer Retailing

The digital revolution has enabled direct-to-consumer (D2C or DTC) retailing. Historically, brands had to sell their products in bulk to retailers or middle men. These were then sold on individually to the end customer. Some consumer brands (especially fashion) have opened up their own retail shops, but mainly, a consumer brand's business model is to sell in bulk to retailers.

This has now changed, and consumer brands are trying to work out what their D2C strategy should be. I have advised a number of global brands and private equity houses on the opportunities for D2C and the complexities this brings to a brand.

Consumer brands are set up as bulk-selling operators with the best marketing teams and brains in any industry. They look after the brand marketing for their products and 'marketing' the product to the end customer.

Retailers, on the other hand, are in charge of 'selling' the product to end customers. The brand has made the end customer aware of their products; the retailer's job is to get the product to the customers.

This means that the skills of a consumer brand revolve around marketing and business-to-business sales. Many of the brands have large sales teams who work with retailers to sell the products to the end customers.

This has led to an interesting challenge for these consumer brands – how can you sell to the end customer directly?

Why consumer brands want to sell direct

First, let us look at why a consumer brand would want to sell directly to the end customer. There are three clear reasons.

Margin: This is of course the biggest driver for most consumer brands to sell directly to the customer. If they sell direct, they cut out the retailer and make a much better margin. This, however, is not necessarily the case when you look at the full cost of selling direct (see the next section)

Customer relationship: The ultimate aim of any retailer is to sell the customer exactly what they want, when they want it. In order to achieve this, you must understand the customer. Selling directly to your customer gives you a relationship with them directly. You can use this to improve your products, ranges and ultimately sell more products.

Control of the brand: When you sell your products through many different retailers and middle men, you run the risk of losing control of your brand image and reputation. Retailers are able to, in essence, do anything they want with your products, which means they could potentially damage your brand. Online is even more important, as a customer can find your assets (images, words, videos etc.) on many websites and apps. If these are of a poor quality or incorrect, this will affect their perception of your brand and ultimately your sales.

Consumer vs customer – my definition

In all my retailing life I have always and unequivocally talked about the 'customer'. I am a pure-bred retailer and I sell products to my customers and ensure my customers are satisfied.

Where does 'consumer' fit into the equation? Here is my explanation: customers consume products. It is as simple as that. In my opinion, a customer is the key person and they consume products – therefore, by default, they are consumers.

The general use of the language tends to suggest that large brands talk about consumers and retailers talk about customers.

This leads me to the first of the challenges for consumer brands selling directly to customers.

Challenges for D2C retail

There are some compelling reasons to sell direct to consumers, but there are many more challenges faced by consumer brands. I will explore the main challenges here.

Consumer vs customer mentality: This is a big topic and not just a substitution of words. As I mentioned before, 'customers consume products', which means there is a different understanding of consumer vs customer. Consumer brands think 'consumer', which is a product focused mindset, whereas retailers think 'customer', which is service and satisfaction-related (i.e., a retailer can sell any brand as long as it is the right product for the customers' wants, needs and desires).

Product-first thinking: This is the second issue. In my vast experience with consumer brands all over the world, I continually find they are working from a product base first. After a few hours with a consumer brand, I can tell you all about their products and how great they are. However, I am often unable to talk about their customer and what the customer wants. This is a big issue with the psyche of a consumer brand, which must change to successfully trade direct to the consumer.

Culture within consumer brands: The culture is set up for sales in bulk to other businesses – it is a business-to-business selling model. Direct to consumer is a one-to-many relationship, where you are selling the same product over and over again. Consumer brands are experienced in nurturing relationships with retailers and selling bulk items to them over a longer time frame.

Size of the D2C operation: A question commonly asked by consumer brands is, what size should the direct business be? 1%? 10%? 50%? There is no set answer, as this depends on your customers' needs and your distribution strategy. It is unlikely that D2C operations will be more than 50% in the near future and I would suggest that they are likely to remain at less than 15% in total. This is due to the fact that the customer likes to shop at retailers and marketplaces for choice – they do not just want to look at your brand, they want to compare more than one brand. A D2C operation cannot do this unless they stock other brands' products and become a retailer.

One-to-many sales model: Moving to a D2C model is moving from one-to-one relationships, to one-to-many. This is a very different and complex operation, where a consumer brand must deal with distributing products in single items to many addresses – adding cost and complexity to their business.

Existing relationships management: There are significant relationships between retailers and consumer brands that have built up over decades. This is a delicate balance and situation for any brand to change – if a brand goes direct, they are taking sales from the retailers and partners who already sell to the end customer. You are unlikely to create a new market of customers when you sell direct. This means that the current distribution channels will not be appreciative of your D2C operation. Any launch and further growth of this must be in consultation with your existing distribution network. If you disrupt this network too quickly you could lose sales very quickly as retailers complete or delist your ranges.

Fulfilment and business systems: Consumer brands have legacy systems and processes, which will need significant upgrading and changing in order to successfully run a D2C operation. From the core enterprise resource planning system, to the warehousing system, to the website build, there will be significant investment and complexity on the journey. The business needs to weigh up the opportunity of D2C and look at the different types of D2C models that work best for them and their customers.

Online marketplaces

I think this is a great point in the book to discuss the world of marketplaces. This challenge is one which all retailers are facing. Amazon is the best known online marketplace in the western world and Alibaba in the eastern world. Both have a similar model and *modus operandi* – they want to take every single customer and retain them!

They are pure retailer killers with one goal: to be the only place for customers to shop, and they have three distinct advantages.

Product range: A marketplace offers a one-place-shop for customers to buy any product they want, easily and with one retailer. They sell almost anything on a marketplace, meaning a customer can just use the marketplace instead of shopping on lots of different retailer and brand websites.

Ultimate convenience: The ultimate convenience to buy all your different products and add to your basket. These can all be bought in one transaction and delivered in one delivery. There is no fuss, no worry about credit card details and you only need to wait for one delivery.

Vast scale: Marketplaces have significant scale, which cross borders and languages. Amazon, for example, has an integrated European delivery network, enabling customers to buy easily and simply from around the world.

Marketplaces have become a major part of the retail landscape with their online market share anywhere up to 90% in some countries and accounting for around 10% to 30% of total ecommerce retail sales.

As a brand you have the choice to sell through a marketplace and there are many benefits to this, but there are also many drawbacks. Part of your D2C strategy must involve a strategic review of the marketplaces and a plan to trade with or without them as part of your overall offer to your customer.

The Dell model

The purpose of this section is to show how different operating models can be employed in the same sector. I want to share a fascinating example from the consumer electronics sector. I will discuss how the Dell model is different from other electronic brands, and the different opportunities and challenges this has presented it with.

There are four main differences between Dell and the other consumer electronics brands:

Retail thinking: Dell built itself as a consumer brand with customer thinking. They set themselves up to sell to businesses, but with the thinking and culture of a retailer selling to their own customers. This meant their D2C operation could run well from the beginning as customers warmed to the customer-first thinking.

Customer first: Dell has a very strong customer-first mentality and the best example of this is their social media listening centre. Dell views customer service as a priority and allows their customers to connect with them on all direct social media, as well as by telephone and mail. This listening centre monitors social media accounts 24 hours a day across the world, and responds to online customer issues in minutes. This is valued by the customer and helps Dell use this information to grow customer loyalty and increase customer satisfaction. They even use the centre to help marketing and sales - they can let the sales and marketing teams know what the social media themes and trends are, and use marketing to capitalise on these events and trends.

All products for all customers: Consumer brands tend to decide which customers 'are entitled to' buy which of their products. This means that some brands actively do not sell some ranges to some customer segments. With the digital world, this does not make sense and Dell do not adopt this mentality. All Dell products are available to all Dell customers - Dell understand that the customer is intelligent enough to know which products are right for them and want to see the full ranges.

One-to-many system: The Dell system is set up for one order to one customer many times over, unlike traditional consumer brands, which are set up to sell one bulk order to one business customer. This means that the Dell system is set up for single invoices per product, something of a challenge when they are selling thousands of items to one business customer. This is an easy technical fix, but their systems and processes are built for one-to-many selling, i.e. to the end customer.

Summary

We have a very exciting future ahead of us as brands look to develop their D2C models. Some brands will develop large D2C operations and others will use the D2C channel as complimentary to the overall omnichannel experience.

A well run D2C channel will be popular for certain types of customers in certain sectors. Brands are still an important part of our social systems, meaning that customers may prefer to shop with the brands directly.

Brands are also the key knowledge source of the products, allowing customers direct access to more detailed and brand-driven information - something that can give the brand a big advantage via D2C over a retailer.

Chapter 6

Omnichannel Performance Indicators

Measuring your trading is a must for any retailer. We have developed a significant amount of data in our businesses, thanks to the growth and development of technology. We hear discussions around 'big data', which focusses on the sheer volume of data retailers now have access to.

This vast amount of data is a blessing and a curse. The fact that you have data is great, but data on its own is useless. You must be able to use the data. You need to analyse the data and from the analysis you need to make insights and from the insights you need to take action.

Definitions

Data: The measures and information you used to understand your business performance and your customer's behaviours

Analysis: The review and manipulation of the data, to be able to understand what it is telling the business

Insights: Drawing trends, hypotheses and conclusions from the analysis of the data

Actions: Making decisions and changing parts of your business process following the insights from the data

PIs: performance indicators

KPIs: Key (i.e. the most important) performance indicators

This is where the complexities of measurement and PIs and KPIs happen. The vast amounts of data mean that a significant amount of resource needs to be employed in the analysis of this data and this resource is usually expensive.

Analysis software is now being used to great effect in many retailers and brands across the world. This is helping the analysts to spend more time developing insights from the data, rather than just finding and crunching the data. Good insights, which are timely, informed and actionable, are then used to drive business decision making.

With the online world, you are able to measure most things, from visits to orders, from marketing campaigns success to social media chatter. This allows you to build a good understanding of your customer segments, which you can use to drive further sales and improve customer satisfaction.

Offline measurement is more complex and this, coupled with the fact that the customer is likely to research and shop both online and offline, creates problems for measurement. There are many companies working on solving this problem, to try and give retailers a complete view of their omnichannel customers.

Using data to inform actions is the key to success here. The more insights you can gain from your data, the better your decision making will be. I always advise retailers to concentrate on a few KPIs and drill down from there into your PIs.

Online KPIs

Online measurement is great because online you can measure most data points. The complexity comes from incorrect integrations and measurement and from a lack of understanding of the main KPIs.

I have a very simple formula for online KPIs:

$$\textbf{Sales} = \textbf{Traffic} \times \textbf{Conversion Rate} \times \textbf{Average Transaction Value}$$

- Sales- the retail value of the sales through your tills online
- Traffic - the visitors to your website/app/mobile site
- Conversion rate - the number of people who placed an order as a percentage of the number of people that visited the website
- Average transaction value - the average value of each order

If you use just one set of KPIs, I suggest you use this one. I fully understand that the world is a lot more complex than this, but these are the key measure and all the rest of the measure flow into these. If one is not at the level you expect, then you can drill down in the data from that KPI.

This formula can be used for forecasting as well as measurement - it is a mathematical formula, which means you can forecast your sales using the three measures.

VARYING COMPLEXITY OF SALES INDICATORS

Measure	Complexity	Details
Sales	Easy	All your activity should be designed to increase the value and number of sales through your online tills
Traffic	Easy	You can increase traffic to your website by increasing your marketing or improving your marketing activities. With the right resources you can easily influence this metric.
Conversion rate	Hard	Conversion rate optimisation is improving your conversion rate gradually, making small changes that take time to develop, implement and see results from. A powerful metric that enables continuous improvement.
Average transaction value	Hard	Improving the average transaction value can take time, but there are also simple promotional and merchandising changes which can improve this, i.e. multibuys, threshold deals, add-ons etc.

There are many different variations on these metrics and the detail you can break them down into is vast. I always advise to keep it simple and you will not go wrong.

If you have vast resources, the better the data, the better the analysis and therefore the more the insight and actions will improve. Make sure you challenge the insights and push through the actions you have made on the basis of the insights.

Offline KPIs

Offline measurement is much more complex. We are unable to measure our customer behaviour easily when they are not online or in store. Customers' shopping journeys span offline and online in many different ways, and the final sales may take place in the store or it may take place online.

That said, the KPIs for offline are in essence the same as online. You want to measure the same type of data, that being:

Visitors – the people who walk into your stores

Sales – the items and transactions sold

Any other measure offline gets more complex, but with the right resources and partners you can measure lots of offline PIs.

Omnichannel KPIs

We have looked at online and offline KPIs – but what does this mean for omnichannel KPIs? This is the challenge for all retailers – how do you measure your business as one?

Customer journeys make this complex. They research on their phones, then they pop into a store and finally they order on the desktop for a collect at store order. They span all your channels in one transaction. This is difficult, but not impossible, to track.

There are currently many retailers tracking their customers' online and offline journeys. Retailers can partner with companies that have mobile data from their customers (i.e. mobile phone companies and Google). This can then be linked to sales data form the stores and the online stores to build a full picture of the customer's journey.

The future of this is exciting, and knowledge and data will grow as technology continues to grow and evolve.

Summary

Measuring your business progress is the key to your success, and there have been many studies that demonstrate this. There has never been a better time for being able to measure a range of variables for a retail business, making the biggest challenge the volume of data, rather than the data itself.

Use the key data and make sure you analyse, gain insights, and take action.

Chapter 7

Digital Marketing Channels

Using digital marketing channels for marketing a physical retail outlet has been common for the last few years, but the overwhelming customer expectation is that they want to shop and buy products online. Therefore, you need an ecommerce website, which is part of your omnichannel strategy to market and grow your business.

An ecommerce website offers global market potential: you can market your product to (nearly) every country in the world and target within that market specific customer segments that you have identified as important to your business.

This will give you the opportunity to sell many more products to new customers and also develop and grow your product range as your customers' needs and desires for your products grow.

The omnichannel approach would mean that you use the website as a transactional ecommerce profit-making business, but also use the website as a 'window' into your store. Your physical store window will be used to market and promote your business. Think of the website front page in the same way – let customers see into your business and make them excited about your brand and your products.

A great marketing opportunity for an omnichannel retailer is to allow the website to give your customers 'sneak peeks' and insights into your business and your plans for the future. You can do this through many methods that are cheap and impactful when you have a great ecommerce site.

The marketing funnel

There is a well-known and understood marketing funnel where you attract customers to your business through awareness and drive them down the funnel to conversion (i.e. purchasing)

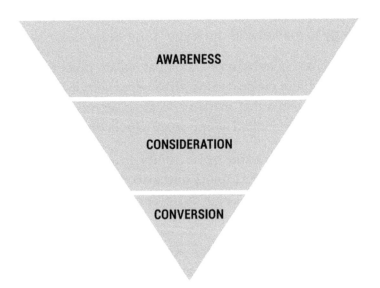

At the awareness stage you concentrate on making your customer aware of your brand. There are many different types of marketing available, such as display marketing,

CRM (customer relationship management) – emails, push notifications etc. – and events.

At the consideration stage, the customer knows that they want a product and they are considering you as an option for the product. Paid adverts such as Google Shopping, retargeting, and affiliates would help here. The customer is engaged, so you need to reinforce the message.

At the conversion stage, the customer is on your mobile site, your app or website. The product page needs to be perfect here and give the customer all the details they need. The call to action should be clear (i.e. an 'add to basket' button) and the checkout should be simple and quick.

Marketing online

There are different forms of marketing online that you need to be aware of:

Search engine optimisation

The basic element to get right from the start is search engine optimisation (SEO). You need to ensure that your website is well-ranked in the search engines, so that when someone types your product or service into Google, you are displayed as one of the first companies on the list offering the product.

This is an important part of the design-and-build phase when you set up a website, and it should also be part of an ongoing strategy to ensure that you are always easily found when current and prospective customers type in your product name.

Search engines are powerful and the larger retailers spend millions on SEO strategy. You will not be able to compete with them directly, but there are many ways you can improve your rankings in much simpler ways.

A few examples would be: making sure the names of the pages reflect the products you are selling; ensuring your website is full of relevant content to your product; having a link-building strategy (where you link to other websites and they link to your website); and building credibility of your brand on the internet – using videos is a great way to engage your customers and build good SEO rankings.

Paid-for advertising

Mainly known as PPC (pay per click), this is advertising on search engines (like Google) and you pay every time a person clicks on your links. This can be successful, but also expensive if poorly implemented.

The best way to approach this is to understand what words your customers search for when they look for your company and then build an intelligent process to capture these searches and visits.

Remember, the aim of a search engine is to give the user the most relevant result for their search. Therefore, the more relevant you make your website and your PPC campaign, the more relevant customers you will receive, and the cheaper those customers will be to acquire.

Social media sites such as Facebook and Linkedin, have started to allow more advertising on their websites, and they can be more relevant for your products. It is important to make sure you put in place a comprehensive strategy for paid-for advertising, alongside the other forms of marketing I have discussed.

Direct advertising and adverts

This is when you set up an advert directly on a website and pay for the placement of this advert. There are many forms of this, with the most common being forums, entertainment sites and popular news sites, which customers visit regularly. It is the same as advertising in a newspaper or magazine, just it is on a screen using different images such as sky scrapers, text boxes and banners.

Affiliate marketing

This is where you allow another website to market your product to their customers in return for a commission payment. The advertiser (your business) would pay a publisher (the business with the customer's information you wish to approach) a commission for referring a customer who ultimately purchases one of your products.

The process can be operated through three main channels:

- Adverts on publishers' sites (they would look the same as a direct advert)

- An email sent to a customer database the publisher owns that has a number of customers that fit your target customer segment profile

- A loyalty programme, where the publisher runs a scheme that offers customer incentives to purchase your products via their website

Marketing an ecommerce website has many benefits over physical marketing:

- Generally cheaper – more cost-effective
- Measurable – you can track the people who look at the advert or read the email and then purchase from you
- It has a wide reach – the world is the customer base
- Complements any offline marketing strategy

An omnichannel strategy needs to adopt a total marketing plan – you must ensure you view the marketing of the physical retail store and the ecommerce website the same; they are different mediums, but the overall theme, messages and brand must be the same. This will ensure that the customer understands your business and knows how all your channels interact as one seamless business.

Delivering total customer experience and service

An omnichannel retail offer will be expected by all customer segments, whether old or young, male or female. A large proportion of the population now uses the internet regularly and a large proportion shops for many different products online.

Offering an ecommerce website will enable you to grow with your customer and help improve their lives. We all know that people are getting more and more pressured for time and having convenient shopping options is very important. Your customers now want to shop 24/7 and they want to shop on their terms and when they want.

An ecommerce website fulfils these needs – the website is open 24/7 and allows them to interact with your business as if they were in your stores, whenever they want to and at their convenience. This will mean your customers will be happier and more satisfied with your business.

An integrated omnichannel operation will enable you to grow your product range more than you can in a physical retail store. In a physical outlet you are limited by space – there are only so many products you can put into the store. Online, your only limit is your brand and what your customers want to purchase from your business.

Any new product ranges that are online-only must complement the core range and adhere to your brand values. You will not succeed if you add products that are not relevant to your customer segments and you will be left with stock that does not sell.

When you set up the omnichannel operations, you should ensure that all your customer data is integrated. A customer does not care what channel they shop in with you, they want to ensure that they are served at the same standard each time. You can use the data from your physical store and your online store to understand how they shop and use each channel – very powerful information for future product planning.

Organisational structure in a digital world

Over the last few years I have seen every organisation progress into and through the digital world. There are many different opportunities to adapt to a digital world and there is no one solution that fits all retailers and consumer brands.

The ideal organisation will become digital first in their strategies, meaning the whole company understanding and using digital to enable customer satisfaction and achieve the company goals.

However, the evolution of organisational structure tends to stick to a familiar course.

Standalone ecommerce/'direct' division or team

In 2006, I joined Dixons group as part of the 'Direct' team. This is when we were selling on desktop sites and we were completely subservient to the physical stores.

The CEO told me, 'The website is a window into our stores', meaning that we were just an online catalogue.

The ecommerce team only is rebranded as multichannel/omnichannel

The omni/multichannel team is then given greater scope of accountability and works more closely with the rest of business, but its sole accountability is for selling via the online channels.

The optimum model – fully integrated across the business

The optimum model is to fully integrate digital into everybody's role across the entire business. This means that job titles don't have the qualifier digital/ecommerce/multichannel/omnichannel in them. The business is structured around the customer, and digital skills are part of everybody's role within the company and the strategy is a digital-first strategy.

The following are common issues for companies as they progress to become a fully integrated digital-first organisation:

- Lack of consistency in direction (hippo – highest paid person's opinion)
- The wider business is unaware of what ecommerce does and is scared of 'digital'
- There is often little accountability and poor communication, due to a lack of digital understanding

Summary

Digital needs to be an integral part of your business. It is not a separate department or channel, it is a way of life, and often the first port of call for your customers. Embrace digital and you will move your business forward quickly and ensure you stay fit to compete.

Chapter 8

Content And Keywords Are Key To Success

Content is the information that you share with your customers and includes all that you say, write, film, produce and the images that you use in your business. One of the most important concepts and understandings that you need as a retailer if you are online is that having good quality, relevant content is an absolute must.

All content needs to be:

- Relevant – ensure your content is relevant to your segments. Ensure the topic is what they are wanting to hear about and that you share this in the right channels

- Timely – some content is timely, i.e. blogs on events that are happening, and need to be shared at a point in time when it will have the most impact

- Good Quality – make sure every piece of content you share with your customers is of good quality and reflects you and your business well

- Engaging – your content needs to engage with your customers and allow them to interact and engage with you

Keywords

When you are developing content, you must use and understand keywords. Keywords are the words that your customers use to find you online, on social media and in search engines.

When you search on a search engine, when you look at any sort of search function on any website on the internet, you need to have a set of keywords that describe your business. These are common to your business across the board and are the descriptive words used to describe you and your business.

In the past, we used to have them clearly showing - if you can imagine a high street, the signs outside shops are in essence keywords. As you walk down the street, you see a greengrocer, butcher, baker - and a candlestick maker in the good old days. When you saw these signs you immediately knew what was inside the shop.

In the same way, you need to have keywords and those keywords that you used to see on a high street need to be online and in all your content.

How to find your keywords

How to find your keywords is probably the question I get asked the most often, and there is no single answer. There are a few places where you can find them.

The first place I would always start is to ask your customers. Your customers are the people that are buying your products and they will have a set of words that they use when they are looking for your products.

You must find out what words customers use when they are looking for you. What do they type into Google or Biadu in the search boxes? Understanding this information will give you a set of words that your customers use to find you.

From this knowledge, you can really funnel down to the exact keywords that you want to be known for and products you are competing for. Again, let' think about a high street and shops. People know what a greengrocer is and they will look down the street to find this shop. So your keywords would say: fruit, vegetables, fresh, available etc.

The key task is to get down to the words that people use to describe your product range and expand those slightly to refine the messages that you are trying to give and the exact products and services that you are trying to sell.

The simple keyword model:

- Ask your customers what words they use to find you and discuss you
- Research the market - look at your competitors and other people that are in your field
- Use the Google keyword tool
- Test the keywords on your market
- Use the keywords in all your content
- Adapt your keywords with time and with new products and ranges

In terms of the number of keywords that you should use, there is no restriction. You can have a million keywords if you want, but it would not work at all if you had that many as this would defeat the object of refining keywords to be 'key'. The ideal number of keywords is probably three to four because people type into Google two, three, four, or five words and your goal is to be those keywords. Having a small number of keywords is important so that everything you do, everything that you write online can have those keywords in. Too many keywords will make writing good content difficult.

It is also important to bear in mind that from a technical point of view, you need to have these words on your website. This is called SEO (search engine optimisation) and best practice suggests that keywords should be in the title and in other parts of the website. This is because Google (and other search engines) will look at these words and see if the website, the blogs and the social media content are all in line. This is important, as searching on Google will show your details and you want to be found for your keywords in this search.

The reality is, if you do not include keywords in all your online and social media channels, no matter how beautiful your site, it will be invisible to your customers.

Tools to help you find your keywords

In terms of a technical process, once you believe you know what your keywords are, after you have spoken to your customers and carried out your research, you can use the keyword tool that is in Google. Anybody can sign up to a Google account; it is simple to open an account and you can search for the 'keyword tool' and it will tell you how to do it. In this tool, Google tells you how many people have searched for your chosen keywords.

For example, if you are a shop selling shirts, you can type in 'shirts' and it will tell you that a few million people each day search for shirts, You do not want to compete with millions of other websites, however. You want to compete with a smaller number of competitors and to do that you need more focused keywords. You could try a couple of keywords together, maybe 'luxury' or 'white shirts'. The keyword tools will tell you the number of people who search for these keywords.

Summary

Finding your perfect keywords is a process of elimination in finding your best keyword combination. It is a combination of what your customer searches for, of what you know about your own business, and then using these keyword tools to see what people on the internet do, what they search for, and the Google keyword tool is probably the best place for that.

Chapter 9

Social Media

Social media has been spearheaded by Facebook and has become the term used to describe the way that we interact socially on the internet, using different types of conversations and discussion mediums. Social media is now extremely important to all businesses across the world, whether they use the internet or not. Your customers will use the internet to talk about your company and interact with your company whether you want them to or not. The customer is now in control of communication about your business and your brand.

You cannot control social media, but you can listen to it and use it to develop your business. Being proactive with social media is very important and needs to be addressed quickly.

It is important to use social media to 'listen' to what is being said about your brand and business. You can form communities of like-minded customers and discuss with them new ideas, products, and deal with any concerns and issues they may have.

There are many different ways to do this, which we discuss later. Not only can you 'listen' to your customers via social media, you can connect with them at any time, wherever they happen to be. This is powerful to keep your customers up to date with what is happening in your business, be it about a problem you need to let them know about (e.g. the website is undergoing maintenance for a couple of hours) or a new product launch that you would like them to attend.

Great use of social media will allow you to interact with your customers and help sell the story of your products and brand. For example, YouTube is a video channel where anybody can upload and view videos. You could use this channel to introduce your brand and company and discuss the latest benefits of your products.

People are now connected to the internet 24/7 and often use mobile devices to connect. These allow many promotional opportunities to be gained while customers are out shopping and in the mood to buy products.

The most important tip for social media is to target the correct media channels and develop an informative and interactive communication strategy. This engages and drives the customers to a deeper understanding of your brand and ultimately drives them to purchase more products from you. The main types of social media include:

- Social media websites - Twitter, Facebook, Linkedin, YouTube and Slideshare are some of the main websites. Using these social media sites will help to make people aware of you and your products and, in some cases, you can advertise directly

- Blogs - blogging is when anybody writes something related to your company and posts it online to create interest and awareness. There are many forms, and they can be adverts, but their main purpose is to build credibility and brand awareness

- Articles – writing an article on your area of expertise and posting it on your website to build awareness and credibility. There are ways to then distribute this further, such as using news hubs.

Summary

- Direct-to-consumer retailing entails both challenges and opportunities
- The customer journey has changed
- Your customers expect you to be everywhere they want to shop, whenever they want to shop
- Increasing your ability to compete means being online
- Use the internet to market your business
- Understand and embrace social media
- Understand omnichannel KPIs
- Deliver total customer experience and service

Part Three

RETAIL PRINCIPLES

Chapter 10

The Retail Standards

There are a few key retail standards that have been adopted and developed over time, which are the foundation of any good retailer.

Standard one – the customer is the most important person in your business

The customer holds the key to every successful retailer, and to master an understanding of your customer there are many processes and procedures you should follow. This part of the handbook follows a logical ten-part flow, which centres around, and begins with, the customer. Based on 25 years of experience and a number of different retail businesses, this handbook will guide you through the journey to make your business customer-focused and realise the potential you have to make your retail business a success.

The main retail standard to master is the customer; the customer should be the centre of your business and everything you do must revolve around that customer. Knowing them, and focussing on them in everything you do, will help you grow your business and your team – The Customer is King.

Standard two – retail is detail

One of the most famous standards in retailing is, of course, 'retail is detail'. This is where the challenge lies. How do you become more detailed and what detail should you focus on?

The answer to these questions is what this handbook sets out to do: to help you start to address and improve your understanding of your customer and the details of running a retail business. Every retailer must focus on the detail and get the detail right the majority of the time. Mistakes happen, but you must learn from them and do not repeat your mistakes. Customers will allow you some mistakes, but too many will turn them away; understanding the detail is a key skill to master in retail.

Standard three – understand the four Ps

This is an old standard but still has validity – most people have heard of the principle from school, college or university. This retail standard will help you understand the overall foundations of a retail business. The four Ps are: product, price, place, promotion. These are the main areas you need to perfect for a customer, to provide the basic foundations of a successful retail business.

1. **Product:** You need products that your customer wants to buy and a product range that will satisfy your customers' needs, wants and desires. The products must also deliver a profit for you to have a successful business

2. **Price:** Price must be consistent across the whole marketing mix and meet all requirements for your

business. You need to price your product range at the correct level for customers to be able to buy your products and for them to gain value from your products. Price transparency is in the customers' hand – they can now see prices for all products anywhere and anytime. This makes setting and maintaining prices an important area to focus on

3. **Place:** You must provide somewhere for your customers to purchase your product, be that a physical store, a catalogue or an ecommerce website; there needs to be a place for the customer to visit (in person or virtually)

4. **Promotion:** Once you have a product – at the right price, in a place where the customer can access it – you need to tell them about this and promote your business and your products. Make sure your customers know that you and your products exist and are available for them to enjoy

I understand that there are more iterations of this, e.g., the 'seven Ps' and others, but I am focusing on the basics – if you get the basics right you will be a good retail business wherever you trade.

Standard four – go the extra mile for your customer

Providing great customer service starts with understanding and knowing your customer (see next chapter); however, knowing them is the start of the journey and, as you have probably realised by now, you need to deliver more than just customer service.

To be successful you must deliver world-class customer service; you must 'go the extra mile for the customer'. This principle is founded on years of experience with customers and working with many different teams that provide customer service. Having a total focus on the customer is the start, but to provide 'world-class customer service', you and your team must continually go the extra mile for the customer, each time delivering just a little more than they expect. Doing this each time you and your team interact with your customers will win them over and make them loyal over a long period of time.

Standard five – location, location, location

We mentioned place above and the final retail standard I will introduce at this stage of your journey is: location, location, location. History has dictated that this is one of the most important factors in the success of a physical store, and still to this day it will have a major impact on your success. The best location of your store will be dictated by your brand and product strategies – i.e. what you intend to sell will affect the location of your store. For example, a supermarket operation needs a car park and a high fashion store needs to be in a high fashion area that attracts the right customers for the store. I would argue that location has less effect now than previously, due to two main factors: the first being the flexibility of the customers, who travel more, to more varied locations, than historically.

Secondly, and most importantly, the internet has changed our shopping habits and will continue to do so. The internet and ecommerce websites have opened up the world of 'non-geographic' retail – a retail world without the need to visit the physical store. The emergence of 'etail' from 'retail' has been the biggest change over the last 20 years and will continue to transform retail over the next 20 years and more.

You will notice that 'etail' has always been a part of the word 'retail'. The journey from retail to etail has been quick, and we need to embrace the world of etail and ensure we understand its effects on our customers, today and in the future. The etail world is growing significantly and with new technologies, such as iPads and M-commerce (using mobile devices to access the internet and buy products), it will continue to change the shape of, and opportunities in, the world of retail.

THE RETAIL JOURNEY

Chapter 11

Know Your Customer

This diagram will appear at the start of the next few chapters and shows the retail journey in a logical order. For this chapter, the customer is at the centre of the circle, and we will be exploring how you can get to know them. You can then move on to the next chapter, which discusses your product. Follow the flow through the rest of the book, using the diagram at the start of each chapter to remind yourself of where you are in the journey and what steps you have already completed successfully.

Who is your customer?

Your customer is the person who buys the products you sell for their end consumption.

Knowing your customer - their lifestyle, habits, likes and dislikes - is the most important element of every successful retailer.

Your customer is the key to your future growth in sales and profits. Understanding your customer will allow your business to grow with your customer and provide them, and potential new customers they bring with them, complete satisfaction for their lifetime.

This is the main focus of the whole journey to improving your retail potential and providing your customers with world-class service.

This section helps you to understand your customer, but the customer is not just mentioned in this chapter – you will find the customer mentioned in every chapter (including the finance chapter) – as they are *the most* important element of your business.

The customer is key to unlocking your retail potential.

'Lifetime value' of a customer

Knowing your customer takes time and effort, but it is worth every second of your and your team's time. Every penny that you invest in the customer will be returned in multiples if you make your customers happy and fulfil their needs.

Remember: a happy customer will tell five people, whereas an unhappy customer will tell 11 people. This is the most varied statistic in retail, but the moral of the statistic is to make your customers happy, and they will shop with you more and will bring new customers to shop with you.

Online, this is magnified and you can argue that a bad customer experience can be shared to 6,000 people (a quote from Jeff Bezos from Amazon). I have had significant experience with large consumer brands who have suffered because of unsatisfactory online customer service.

Social media has become the *de-facto* place for customer complaints (Twitter, WeChat, Facebook, forums etc.). If you look at best practice examples, a good brand will respond to a customer post in 15 minutes and this is a standard being adopted by the world's best brands and retailers.

Unfortunately, many brands pay lip service to social media customer service and are damaging their reputation on a daily basis. Imagine that a customer is on their journey researching a product and they come across a tweet that says, 'This is the worst product I have ever used'. If this post is not responded to by the brand or retailer, this will become bad PR and will negatively influence the customer's journey.

Once you have a happy loyal customer, you can guarantee that the people they tell will become loyal new customers and they in turn will recommend more potential customers to you. We all like to moan, but we also like to tell our closest friends and family a great story about good customer service, and this personal recommendation helps to grow a good quality and loyal customer base.

In retail, there is a concept called 'lifetime value' of a customer – this means looking at your customer over a long period of time. Think of your customer over the next five or ten years of visiting your shops and websites. Think about how easy it would be to sell those customers more products and services once they have tried you and liked your service and products. Making a customer loyal over the long term is much more important than selling them one or two products.

For example, if you run a clothes shop selling ladies fashion, your perfect customer would be the lady that buys a few garments every new season (and also tells her friends how good your products are). If there are two seasons a year and she buys a top and a skirt each time at £100, in one year she spends £200; in five years she has spent £1,000 with you.

When she walks in for the first time, make her the most important person in the shop – look at her as a potential lifetime value of £1,000 plus. How differently would you treat a £1,000 shopper versus a £100 shopper? How would you set up your store and train your team to look at each customer as a 'lifetime value', not just a quick one-day transaction?

Here I have another example of 'lifetime value' for a local wine store. A customer will, on average, buy a case of wine every three to four months. That means that an average customer will buy 48 bottles of wine in a year. At £7 for the average bottle of wine, that is a potential £336 of sales and with a margin of 35%, that is a potential £117 gross margin.

When you first meet a customer you should view them as a long-term customer with a margin value of £117 a year. This value of £117 per year is what you can view as their lifetime value – each year you will make £117 from this customer if you keep them loyal.

Loyalty and lifetime value

Gaining a customer for their lifetime is an ongoing process, which can be implemented in many ways. The main idea is to think about the total value the customer will bring to your business and use some of the profits from that regular customer as an incentive or discount to 'earn' their loyalty.

You will need to 'pay' for the loyalty of the customer via discounts or other ways, but all of these will cost your business and you will need to make an investment into customer loyalty. To keep them loyal, why not give them a special offer: on their first visit why not give them a 20% discount on the first bottle of wine (cost to you £1.40)?

Tell them that if they come back you will give them a further discount or offer, e.g. 15% off the next bottle (cost to you £1.05). The third time they come back, you offer them a volume deal – such as 10% when they buy three bottles (cost to you 70p per bottle). You then offer 10% ongoing for the customer.

Let's add up the costs and profit in this example (I ignore taxes here for simplicity):

Visit	Retail Price £	Discount £	Cost price (65%) £	Margin £	Margin %
First	7	1.40	4.55	1.05	15%
Second	7	1.05	4.55	1.40	20%
Third	7	0.70	4.55	1.75	25%
Average	7	1.05	4.55	1.40	20%
Average of 48 bottles with 10% off	336	34.65	218.40	82.95	25%
48 bottles @ 20% off	336	50.40	218.40	67.20	20%

In this example we have retained the customer by offering a discount, but this is not the only way to view lifetime value.

The total value of the discount in this example is: £34.05 (£117- £82.95).

This 'discount' could be given as a number of benefits to the customer, such as a free half-case each year (six bottles would cost you £27.30), a free wine-tasting event every six months, or a number of free wine-related products (e.g., free glasses and decanter) every few months.

The example above is designed to help you put a financial value on each customer and give them special offers and events to gain their loyalty and make you the best return over time. It shows that the '£100 customer' should not exist in your culture, your team's culture or anywhere in your business. Thinking 'lifetime value' is where you need to start your journey today.

Please take a moment to visualise the lifetime customer of your store or your potential store – start to build up an image of them in your head. Use the example above with your products and figures – what benefits could you start to offer your customer to make them a lifelong customer of your store?

Implement a loyalty scheme

A loyalty scheme is any type of programme or event that allows you to interact with your customer on a regular basis, to gain ideas, opinions and views on your store. It involves offering the customer something in return for their time and ideas – from money off, to free tea and coffee. Implementing some form of scheme that allows you to interact with your customer on a regular basis, to understand them better now and in the future, is important. This type of interaction is vital for continued success and growth of your retail business.

A loyalty scheme will allow you to understand what they like and dislike; what they want and do not want. How useful would it be to know which products you should buy for your customers and what not to buy? If you find out this information, you can buy exactly what they want, when they want it and know the price they are willing to pay for it.

A great example of a full service loyalty scheme can be seen at Tesco. Tesco founded the Clubcard to help their understanding of customers' purchasing habits, so they could market more products and sell more products and services to their customers. This was highly successful and has helped the company become the UK's largest retailer and the third biggest retailer in the world.

Their scheme is very simple: each time you shop at Tesco and Tesco.com you swipe a card that adds to your personal database of information. Tesco then knows what you bought at what price and when. In return you get vouchers and money off future shopping. Tesco adds this data to your personal information and can build up a very powerful image of each customer. This allows them to target your personal interests and promote products to you that they know you will want to purchase.

Obviously the Clubcard scheme is very expensive to implement, but any retailer can still offer a scheme. I talked earlier about the wine shop discounting, which you could implement in any store as a tiered discount model, but you could easily implement a basic loyalty card online and offline.

Gathering customer data allows for analysis of the customers' buying patterns and preferences. This data can be used to buy your next range or promote good sellers/poor sellers or cross-sell a related product. This customer data is factual and allows you to build a real picture of your customer and what they buy from you, in what quantities, at what prices and times. This data can feed all the future planning of your business, from the next season's range to next year's promotional and marketing plan.

A good loyalty scheme would need to:

- Gather customer data – as much as possible, but a name and email address is a good start

- Record your customers' purchases – if you are able to tag their purchase on your system and find out what a customer is buying, you can build a valuable database of their buying patterns

- Analyse the total sales data – you can analyse which products are selling in total (not by individual customer). This data can be used for promotions and marketing plans, and also the buying plans for the next period

- Analyse the individual customer data – once you have the data at customer level, you can analyse what each customer is buying. This data can be used for promotions and marketing to that specific customer segment; if they bought a product once, they are likely to buy it again

- Make the customer feel happy – offer a discount, VIP events or special offers, so that the customer feels valued and continues to shop with your business

Know your customers' habits

This is one area where consumer brands lead the way. In my experience, consumer brands know their customer intimately and are able to tell you more than you need to know about your customer. This information (power) is being used by brands to trade directly with customers online and is changing the whole way the retail world and brands operate.

To understand your customer and be able to sell the products they want, at the price they want to pay, you need to 'get under the skin' of your customer – really understand what makes them buy your products.

To do this you need to find out about their lifestyle. Ask them, directly or indirectly, what their interests, sports and hobbies etc. are. Use this understanding to model a picture of their lives – look for trends in the information. Maybe most of your customers like cookery, golf, Formula 1 or painting – if so, make sure your products and stores attract people with those interests.

For example, if your customer likes cookery, and you run a book shop, make sure the cookery section is clearly defined and that you promote the books and use special offers or events to make your customers happy. You can even partner with local shops or service providers to offer an even better service to your customer. For example, you could offer a discount with the local fruit and vegetable shop, or have a joint themed evening of cooking classes, with parcels of ingredients ready packaged for your customers to take away with your books.

To gather customer information, use your resources:

- Your team and your stakeholders - good team members will always interact with your customers, so ask your team what they know about your customers' lifestyles. There will be many areas of your customers' lifestyles that your team will know already; you need to help them collate these and discuss how these can help your business

- Hold VIP events or local events - offer some free drinks, nibbles and a discount in exchange for their time completing a short questionnaire. The questionnaire should cover all areas of the customers' lifestyle and be detailed enough to allow you to analyse the results and information

- Set up a customer database - collect your customers' email details when they purchase an item and email them a short questionnaire. Again, the questionnaire needs to be detailed, but online it needs to be user-friendly and take up no more than five minutes of their time

- Observe your customers:

  ⌃ If you run a local store you should know your customers and probably live near to them. You will already know what your customers' interests are - all you need to do is write them down. Take time out to think about what you already know about your customers

  ⌃ If you are not local, make the time to observe the customers in your store; spend a couple of weeks watching the customers shop and interact with your team. Vary the days and times you do this and don't be afraid to talk to the customers yourself

⅄ If you run an ecommerce website, you can employ research tools that can track your customers' movements into, around and out of your website. Tools like Google Analytics are a great start to understanding more about your customers

⅄ Make sure that you employ data capture of their details to ensure you can understand and contact your customers in the future

Understand where and how your customer shops

Finding out other places where your customer shops will tell you the other types of retailers they like and the type of products they buy. This information is powerful, as it helps you to understand what you should offer your customers more or less of.

There are many types of products you can offer:

- Similar/complementary products to your competition

- Products that you know your competitors do not offer, yet you know your customer wants

- Products that your competitors offer, but you are able to improve the product or service for your customer

For example, if you run a grocery chain, and you know your customers always shop at the local health-food shop, you may consider selling more organic food, or make sure your customers know that you already sell these products.

Finding out how your customer shops is very important. The times of just a physical store and maybe a catalogue have moved on significantly. Customers now use 'apps' on their smartphones, mobile phones, telephone ordering and the internet to research and buy products. You need to know how your customer shops now and in the future. For example, if you serve the under 25s market, you must have the latest app to enable them to find your products, view them and order from them if necessary. Likewise, if you serve the over-55 market, a great physical store experience with an informative website is a must (Fact: 'Silver Surfers' are the largest growing community on Facebook and for using the internet).

To find out where and how your customer shops:

- Ask your customers - ask them how they like to buy your products and where they buy them from currently
- Ask your team - a good, customer-focused team will interact with your customers and can easily find out this information from your customers
- Observe the customers - watch what bags they have with them and what labels they are wearing. See if they have a smartphone or mobile phone when they are in your store
- Hold focus groups - hold a number of focus group for a select customer segment, and ask them where they shop and how they shop. Find out how

they like to shop now and how they think they will shop in the future

Build an image of your customers

The purpose of this section is to build up an image of your customer - as clear and detailed an image as possible. You want to be able to describe every element of your customer and this will drive benefits in all parts of your business.

You are very likely to have a number of different customer segments, maybe four or more. With each type of customer segment, build up an image and name your customer segments. Sit down with your team and your data to visualise what the types of customers are and name them - a person's name can be used to help make this process real.

For example, you may find that many of your customers are young males in the 25-35 age range and they visit your shop every evening around 6pm. You will immediately start to build up an image of these men, what they wear, the speed they shop, the types of products they buy. You could name this group 'young male shoppers' or even a person's name that you know fits your desired customer segment.

Once you have defined your customer segments, you can then apply all areas of your business to focus on giving these segments world-class customer service. Give the customer segments the most perfect customer service that you can offer them, which they will appreciate and value.

Don't be afraid to be too niche ('niche' is a small defined group with similar characteristics) with your segments - the more specific the segment, the easier it is to buy products for them and market to them. You could find your customer segment is even tighter than the example above and you notice that these men always wear suits, buy ready meals and use credit cards. You could tighten the name of the segment – 'young professional male convenience shoppers'. This process will help you define every part of your business and enable you to build a product range and process to satisfy your customer segments.

To build an image of your customer segment:

- Analyse your data – have a look through your existing databases of email addresses, names, orders and all other information you have at customer level

- Ask your teams – have a 'brainstorm' with your customer-focused teams to describe and visualise your customer segments

- Build a visualisation of the segments – look at their age, sex, profession, style, attitude, address, interests, etc.

- Name the segments -- this could be a real person's name if it helps give a real image

- Survey the customers – in return for a discount or special offer, most customers will answer a five-minute questionnaire, where you can gather all this information

In order to segment your customers accurately it is useful to sit down as a team and discuss the different types of customers you know.

FASHION STORE CUSTOMER SEGMENTATION

What do we know about our customers?	Results of questionnaires and surveys	Key trends	Customer profiles
• Customer data – from the systems • Customer feedback • Staff feedback • Sales trends in our area or market	• 50% of respondents had shopped at a local high street fashion store in the last six months • Most had three holidays a year • 20% never bought online • 35% only came to the store to browse	• Quality • Time rich • Cash rich • Like to make a considered buying decision • Research, but do not buy online	• 50yr+ females • Retired, but busy • Mostly with grandchildren • Value the good things in life
• As above	• As above	• Fun • Time poor • Relaxation • Entertainment • Designer brands • Online shoppers	• 25–45yr males • Work in the city • Commute daily • Like good restaurants • Regularly buy designer clothes

In this example you can see that this fashion store has two distinct, but similar, customer segments. Both value quality and fashion, but they have differing priorities and buy over different time (i.e. the first group take its time, whereas the second group is spontaneous).

Once you have the customer segments defined, draw and describe them - maybe on the wall or in your company internal documents. Make sure all your teams know who your customer segments are and what they look like.

This information should then be used every minute of every day, in every department - your whole business should now revolve around these customer segments.

You buy for these segments, market to these segments, merchandise to these segments, set your promotional strategies for these segments - these are the focal points for your business and the reason why you are in business - nothing else matters, only these customers and serving them the best you possibly can.

Summary

- Understand the 'lifetime value' of a customer
- Know your customers' habits - visualise your customers
- Understand where and how your customers shop
- Implement a loyalty scheme

Chapter 12

Know Your Product

The product is the physical item or service that you sell to the customer in return for value exchange (usually money paid to your business).

The product is the main element of the customer's journey - being the reason they interact with you. A customer only ever visits a store (online or offline) to fulfil a need, desire or want - no matter how great your customer service and marketing is, a poor product will ultimately mean the end of the business.

Making sure you have the correct products and product range for your customer segments is the next step in the journey.

If you are reading this book as a consumer brand, you are undoubtedly very aware of your products and their USP. I urge you to read his chapter (at speed) but think about how your product is really fulfilling the needs, wants and desires of your customers. Also think about how you can solve these needs, wants and desires on your direct offer to your customers.

Decide what you want to sell

In the previous chapter, we built up a view of your customers and segmented them. We now use that basis to build a product range for those customer segments. Now you know your customer (or your potential customer) you can develop and design a range targeted to your customer segments. Finding out what your customer wants from a product and product range, alongside their needs and desires, will allow you to develop a product and service that fulfils those needs and desires.

To develop your product range, you need to perform a thorough assessment of the market, your skills and your interests.

When you assess the market, look for everything that meets your customer segment's needs. You can retail almost anything: fashion, food, wine, books, cars, CDs, cigars, plants - anything that has been manufactured needs to be retailed at some stage in its cycle to reach the end customer.

Source the product for that niche

Once you have chosen your product range, one that is based on your understanding of your customer segments, you need to get to know and understand what makes your product unique - what the benefits are of your product versus your competitors.

Why should a customer buy your product versus that of your competition? Is yours exclusive? New? Better quality? Cheaper? Personalisable? Part of a theme or collection? Fashionable? Practical?

You must understand what your product (or potential product) offers your customers that is different - understand your product's unique selling proposition/point (USP).

A USP is the general term that describes why your product is for sale and what your customers will receive when they buy your product. The easiest way to think of this is: what are the benefits of the product to your target customer segments?

All products are different in some way, even generic products can be retailed differently, with different retail propositions and services - again, understanding your customer segment will drive the USP for your products.

To know your product:

- Go out and research - walk around your local high street or shopping centre. Find out what is in the market, what interests you, what your customers want, need and desire, what is missing or what products you could improve

- Use the internet – you can sit at home for hours and scan the internet for current products and new products – look at websites from different countries for latest trends and niche products that may not be available in your country

- Talk to your customers – find out, from your customers, what they would like to buy, what products are missing in their lives and then research to see if you can provide these – you may even invent a new product based on this research

Plan the sourcing strategy

Sourcing (also known as the supply chain) is the process by which you find, manufacture or produce the products you wish to retail. This could be as simple as finding a local wholesaler or as complex as sourcing the raw materials and manufacturing your own products.

Part of the getting to know and planning your product is understanding the sourcing strategy – the process where you work out how to get the finished product to your retail outlet/warehouse. This could go back as far as production and you could be part of designing and producing the product yourself or outsourcing the production.

Developing the whole supply chain is a normal strategy for new technology products, such as FreshMax Shirts (a fabric technology company and online retailer), where we worked with an outsourced manufacturing partner to design the fabric, source the raw materials, weave the fabric, design the shirts, cut and make the shirts and dispatch to our warehouse.

As a consumer brand looking to sell direct, you must think about this area. I have worked with most global consumer brands over the last few years, and a big mental and physical shift is needed. A consumer brand is used to selling large numbers of items in volumes to a few retailers or distributors. Once you start selling direct to consumers, you need to think 'one-to-many', where many customers order just one item, and you have to ship this accurately and on-time every time.

Most sourcing for retailers is much simpler and involves finding a wholesaler, distributor or warehousing partner. These partners could buy the products in large quantities direct from the manufacturers and sell them on to retailers in smaller, more manageable quantities.

Warehousing and distribution

There are many ways to find a suitable distribution and warehousing partner – the easiest way is to research on the internet which businesses serve your particular sectors, e.g. wine suppliers, shirt distributors, fruit wholesalers, etc.

A great way to find new partners is through trade fairs. These are held throughout the year and specialise in your particular industry and foreign trade bodies, such as UK Trade and Investment (UKTI), which offer support and help for businesses wishing to trade internationally.

Good sourcing will be in line with your values and principles. It is important to bear in mind the brand image and philosophy when you are arranging your sourcing. This is especially important if you plan to appeal to a customer type that values fair trade or organic farming. This is also true for sourcing products from middle men - you must ensure that the whole supply chain is ethical, safe and adheres to your values.

The final part of sourcing is ensuring that you will be able to get your products to your customers. Make sure that whatever sourcing strategy you use, you are able to get the quantities you need, at the price you want, when the customers want to make the purchase.

Distribution and warehousing are the final part of the sourcing process and you need to decide if you will do any of these activities within your company or if you will outsource these to the specialists. There are pros and cons to doing your own warehousing and distribution, and this needs to be understood at the planning stage. Most small retailers will leave this area with the middle men, who have the scale and resources to warehouse and distribute the products.

Planning the sourcing strategy involves:

- Finding out how your product comes to market now - assuming the product exists today, you can easily research the supply chain that currently exists and adopt this process if it works for your product

- Using your existing networks and contacts - you are already connected to people in business, such as your accountant and your bank manager. Use your connections to find out how other companies source products and where they source them from

- Joining networks and trade bodies - if you do not yet have a big network or you wish to learn more, you will find that most sectors of the retail industry have trade bodies or buying groups that can help you source your product; research these groups and make connections into these groups

- Planning your distribution and warehousing – once you have the product sourced, you need to ensure that you can get it to your customers. You may order in small quantities, have frequent deliveries, and have a warehouse or ship direct from the supplier. All of these are possible, but must be reviewed and planned in line with your customers' needs

Set the pricing strategy

Setting the pricing strategy is an important part of developing your customer offer and your business values. The pricing policy of a retailer will not only affect the profits and sales, but also the perception of the brand and retailer. For example, if I said Pound Stretcher and Harrods to you, you would immediately know that one is going to have low-cost retail prices and one will have more expensive retail prices.

Your pricing should reflect your business values, but also needs to be competitive and make you a profit – after all, we are in this business to make money and we must make sure we sell the majority of our products for a higher price than we bought them for. Remember that we are now in the world of transparency where the customer can research your prices anytime, anywhere – you are no longer able to hide your pricing and you must ensure that the customer clearly understands your prices, both online and offline.

Setting the pricing strategy should also reflect your plans for promotions and markdowns. Some products are known to be discounted often or will be in the end-of-season sales, but you may not want to have much promotional activity with prices (think high fashion - where they have very few sales and promotions on the pricing until the end of the season).

Establish a pricing strategy that provides the customer with the value and quality that they desire and are prepared to shop with you to receive. Go back to your customer segments and understand what they are willing to pay for your particular product and service.

To set a pricing strategy, consider the following options:

Price to make a profit: You must make sure that you have a pricing strategy that makes a gross margin, and that this gross margin should cover the overheads and make an overall profit (gross margin is the sale revenue, less tax, minus the cost of the product that you paid the supplier)

Price for your market: Set your prices in line with your competition, understand where your customers shop and price accordingly

Price for promotions and markdowns: Make sure you set the price to take into account any promotions and any markdowns you may wish to (or be forced to) implement. Supermarkets use a 'loss leader' strategy where they will purposely make a loss on some products in order to attract you to the store and buy more of their range

Set a gross margin target: There are two ways to do this:

1. Set and calculate a percentage margin that you wish to achieve for each product or range, e.g. my business wants to make 40% margin on all shirts.

   This helps the buying process and negotiations, as you can work back from what retail price you wish to sell the product at, and therefore what the maximum buying price will be.

   For example, we wish to sell our shirts for £50 (excluding tax) and I want to make 40% margin to cover my costs (for example, my high street location) – I need to make £20 gross margin, so the maximum I can buy the product for would be £30.

1. Set a mark-up ratio or percentage you want to achieve for each product or product range, e.g. I would like to make 100% mark-up on the buying price.

   For example, I buy a shirt at £20 delivered to my warehouse. I will then sell this for a minimum of £40. If £60 is the minimum retail price, £30 is the mark-up I need to make per item to cover costs and make a profit, so £30 will need to be what I bought it for.

Design and develop the ranges

Once you have established your product area, your pricing strategy, your quality values and your brand values (see later chapter on branding), you can develop your product range.

Developing the product range involves taking time to plan what products you will sell from your desired product category. You will need to develop a product range that achieves what your customers would like and achieves the best profits and value for your business.

Think about the range as a customer segment – what will they want to see in the range? How will you lay out the range? Will it be a seasonal product range? Look at the range in total. For example, if you decided to sell laptops, think about the full range and all the accessories and related products you will need; with a laptop you will need a mouse, camera, carrying-case and maybe even a printer. Providing the customer with a total experience will be beneficial and lucrative if you give the customer a full service offer of products and related products.

To create and develop the range:

- Ask your customers – hold product reviews and focus groups. Sit down with a few customers and discuss the ideas, even show them a few diagrams/videos/images of what the products will look and feel like

- Ask the experts – work with creative product designers to focus the range on exactly what your customers would like

- Manage the total margin – think about a product range in total and make sure you achieve the overall margin you need. For example, you may have loss-leaders to drive footfall or you may wish to have all products making roughly the same margins

- Manage additional products and cross-sales – providing a full service offer of products is important for success. In the laptop example you may make more margin from the accessories than you do from the laptop sold alone

- Vary the range – think about a full range offer. You may be known for high-quality shoes, but you could also sell shoe polish, shoe laces, socks and even shoe racks. Make sure the range does not creep too much, but added products that complement your range are an easy way to increase sales and profits

Summary

- Decide what products you want to sell
- Plan the sourcing (supply chain) strategy
- Set the pricing strategy and policy
- Establish your quality values
- Design and develop the ranges

Chapter 13

Establish Your Brand And Niche

Establishing your brand and finding your niche follow on from understanding your customer segments, and works alongside developing your product.

As a consumer brand looking to sell directly to the end customer, you will of course be experts in your brand and niche, but you need to think about this as a retailer. Make sure you 'speak' customer in all you do - a challenge for most brands that speak 'sales' and volumes.

Your niche is the area of the market in which you operate, and this can be as narrow as 'retailer of the best flowers to people who are getting married' or 'retailing shoes to the city worker' or as wide as 'selling good fruit and vegetables to my local market'. A niche allows you to develop a very strong marketing campaign, and enables you to really understand your customer segments - the more defined the niche, the easier it will be to retail to your customers, and the easier it will be to make money.

Your brand is your image and values - it is the way you act, communicate and the way your business is perceived. It is what your business 'stands for' and is reflected in every single part of the business - from the name of the company, the colour of the logo, the type of bags, to the way your team interacts with your customers and suppliers.

Find your niche in the market

It takes time to find out where you 'fit' into the market. As we discussed in the previous chapter, you need to find a product range and establish your niche for that product range.

Finding a niche in the market means researching the part of the market that interests you and your customers, and breaking that down to a defined section. Understanding what the USP of your product is in the market, and how that translates into a recognisable niche for your customers, will help you define your niche.

This part of the niche development is focused on the customer side of the equation - you need to look at your chosen product and product range from the eyes of your customers and establish what they like about your product and how they would see that as a niche in the market.

I talk of a narrow and small niche because this is much easier for small companies to start with, but very successful large companies adopt this exact same process. Apple has a very clear niche, for easy-to-use 'gadgets' that are 'cool' to own - this is a now a very large niche, but nevertheless this is their niche.

Finding your niche in the market works alongside the product development process and, as such, you follow a similar process:

- Go out and research the market - walk around your local high street or shopping centre. Find out what market niches there are for your product. How do customers currently see your product in the market and where do they purchase these products from now?

- Use the internet to find where your niche would work - have a look at where the product is currently sold and what the market looks like - is there a clear niche that you can see for your product?

- As a customer, think of what your niche would be defined as and what you would need to offer the customers. For example, if you were a florist and said your niche was 'selling flowers' you would find hundreds of companies doing this on every street corner and all over the internet space. If, however, you find your customers are normally people who are attending weddings or parties, you could set your niche as 'retailer of the best flowers to people who are getting married'. This helps you target very specific people with a high-quality tailored service just for them, at the time they need to use your products

- Talk to your customers – find out from your customers what they see as a good market niche and what products they would like to see in this market

Develop your brand and brand values

What is a brand? Your brand is the identity of your business and your products, and often includes physical words, colours and logos. Most of the brand is intangible, and therefore hard to understand. This section talks you through an understanding of what a brand is and gives you a practical process to follow in order to establish and develop your brand.

Your brand and the values your brand stands for span every part of your company. As such, the brand must be thought through and developed to a very detailed level. This is part of the process to grow and develop your business over time, but you must start with a vision of what the values are and this is where the brand journey begins.

Your brand is 'living and breathing' and, as such, needs to be treated with care and allowed to grow and develop as your customers and your team grow and develop.

Your brand is in every part of your business, from the culture and ways of working, to your logo and your packaging. It can be seen inside all the people in your business and in all the products you sell.

Take time to understand your customer segments first and develop the products for these customer segments. Then, work on your niche to identify where you 'fit' in the market. Once these processes are in progress, you can then start to develop the brand around these.

The brand values are sets of statements that will help you, your team and your customers 'feel' the brand you have created. These values will drive your identity and help establish your USP in your niche.

Develop the brand 'voice' and 'imagery'

Once you have created the brand and the brand values, you will also be in the process of creating the images for your brand. This is where you can develop ways to help your brand live and breathe and come alive in your team.

Once the brand values are established, you and your team must consistently 'talk' with the brand language and the brand voice. This means all communications from now on will be in line with your brand values and images. You will have a certain tone of voice, a certain colour scheme and certain images that represent your brand.

A great brand is known for very simple execution - we all know the Apple logo, we know who owns the golden arches logo and we know which sports company uses a tick logo. Of course, this has also taken many years of development and a huge global presence but, as we have shown with FreshMax, a small business can build a great brand and imagery.

Branding will cover every part of your business, such as:

- Physical branding - name, logo and colours
- Iconography and everlasting logos (e.g. the Nike tick)
- Collateral - bags and labels
- Communications - email signatures, business cards, letterheads, email templates and website formats
- The 'way' you communicate with your customer segments (happy, confident, clear, succinct, etc.)
- The service experience – the bags you use, the fitting rooms, and the customer service on offer

  This will also become relevant when you start to create and understand your online content. The images and words used need to be developed from the core and deployed online in a coordinated way. This is discussed in the 'Market Your Product and Brand' chapter.

Decide on channels of operation

The channel of operation is the place in which you will do business with your customer; this will be affected by your brand values and your brand values will be influenced significantly by your place of operation.

There are two main channels of operation: offline (physical locations) and online. Offline are the locations that we have been using to retail products for hundreds of years. We now have many more exciting options than the local high street, but they all consist of a physical presence of products and a team to physically sell these products.

The location of the store affects the brand and the types of customers that use your store and these must be aligned.

The main physical store options are:

- High street
- In-town shopping centre
- Secondary high street location (just off the main shopping area)
- Out of town – retail park
- Out of town – supermarket/hypermarket
- Out of town – stand-alone store
- Drive-through outlets
- Motorway services and travel stations
- Industrial parks (near offices and office workers)

All of these locations are tried and tested retail outlets; some will be relevant to your business and others will not. There will always be a number of options that you can use, and you may choose more than one channel of operation.

Online retail consists of an ecommerce website where customers can see your products online and purchase them for delivery to their home or office. Online is also expanding into different offerings such as:

- Online ecommerce site
- Auction Site
- M-commerce – shopping using your mobile phone
- Apps – using apps on your smartphone to shop anywhere at any time
- Social media

All retailers should now offer customers both online and offline – this is called omnichannel and this is where retailers must move to in the future in order to be competing successfully with other retailers (especially the multi-national larger retailers).

Omnichannel retailing is normally described as retailing through a number of distribution channels, such as a store, a catalogue and via an online presence.

Your choice of channel is determined by:

- Product – the characteristics of the product will mean a certain channel will be applicable or not. For example, is the product perishable? Of high value? Needs to be tested or tried on?

- Customers – how do they want to shop for your product and service? For example, can they travel out of town? Do they have a smartphone? etc.

- Competitors – you need to sell your products in a similar way to your competition, unless your USP is a different sales channel. Customers tend to shop for similar products in similar ways so you need to have at least one channel of operation that is the same as your competition

- Costs to retail – Understanding your gross margins and the cost of retailing via a certain channel is very important to your profit line. For example, does your business model, in particular your margin, allow for an expensive high street position? Do you need to offer lower prices? Do you offer high personal service?

- Accessibility - understanding how accessible your channel is to your customer segment. Do your customers need parking? Do your customers have internet access?

- Experience - you need to remember your values and how you want your brand to be experienced by the customer segments. Do your customers want a particular experience from your retail channel? Do they expect quick simple service?

Finding the correct channel of operation will be achieved over time and most retailers will adopt a number of channel options - omnichannel. Successful retailers are now embracing all channels and a mix of online and offline is by far the most successful model in the current retail market.

Summary

- Find your niche in the market for your customer segments
- Develop your brand and brand values
- Develop the brand 'voice' and 'imagery'
- Decide on your channels of operation

Chapter 14

Build A Team
To Compete

Building a high-performing team that acts as one and grows your business is the key to providing your customers with the best experience your business can possibly provide. Each person in your team has a role, which is extremely important to the achievement of satisfaction for your customers. All your team members need to know their purpose in your team and how that helps achieve customer satisfaction. The first area to develop is a customer-focused culture.

Develop a customer-focused culture

Culture underpins the entire business and helps your team understand how to act and behave when they are part of your business. Culture looks at the values the business wishes to stand for, and is closely related to your brand, your product and your niche. Defining your culture is where the journey begins.

Focusing completely on the customer segments you have defined and understanding your niche will underpin the process to define your culture. Once you have defined your culture, you need to implement practical plans to instil this in your teams, and make it become a way of life in your business - a way of operating that everybody naturally adheres to and one, which represents your business in the way you would like it represented.

Recruit a high-performing team

Once you have a defined set of values and an understanding of the structure of your business, you can start to develop and recruit a team.

The starting point of the journey is a defined set of roles. Based on the structure of your business, whose aim is to service the customer segments, define each of the roles you need in your business. A job description is the obvious starting point and a standard job description can be used for all roles.

All the roles should be part of a structure that fits the business needs and services the customer.

Omnichannel structures

A great challenge is how to structure your omnichannel teams. This is an evolving challenge for all consumer brands and retailers. Digital, ecommerce and the internet have all taken over as major parts of your customers' lives.

Your business structure must adapt to this change and how you adapt depends on your business needs. Most retailers and consumer brands will want to have an integrated team – one which looks after online and offline together. This makes sense as the customer sees no difference in your brand online or offline.

To achieve this is complex, but a strategy must be implemented to address this for now and in the future.

Train the team

Training should start on day one, and in a high-performing business will continue forever. The first day of a new team member's career with you should start with a basic introduction to the company: the products, the team and, most importantly, an introduction to who your customers are and how they should interact with them.

An important session for all your team members will be a 'culture training' session. This should happen in the first few weeks and take the new team members through the company values and explain what they mean and how they are applied in your business.

Training needs to become an embedded way of life, and your team members should want to continually develop themselves; if they develop themselves, then your company will also develop. Offering training programmes is a great way to build a team spirit and also help improve the overall competence within the business.

One way to find out what training a person needs, and keep them striving for high performance, is through a performance development review process, in which you appraise your team member's performance on a regular basis (maybe every six months).

This serves many purposes:

- Reviewing the past six months' performance
- Setting objectives for the next six months
- Reviewing training and development opportunities
- Receiving feedback as a team member's manager

To develop a high-performing team you need to:

- Hold a short induction on day one for all new team members – cover the basics of the business, the 'domestics' (where the toilets are, when the breaks are etc.), the health and safety rules and introduce the customer segments to the new team members

- Set the new team members a first few weeks' training and induction programme to ensure they have all the necessary connections and training they need to perform a great job

- Hold a culture training session with every team member in the first few weeks – make sure they understand your company's values and how they should embrace these values

- Set up a continual performance development process – every six months review the performance of your team and set new objectives and training plans

Communicate with the team

Communication with the whole team is important – from communicating the vision, to communicating the daily sales and trading performance. In general, every person in the business should be fully up-to-speed with what is happening and how these issues affect themselves, and more importantly, your customers.

Communication starts with sharing the vision for the business at the outset – your team needs to know why you are in business and what you are trying to achieve. Understanding the vision enables every team member to understand what they are doing to help achieve this vision and how they can change things if they are not working towards this vision. Having a vision, and common goals, helps bring teams together and bridges gaps between team members who may not understand what the other team members' job roles are, and how they all interact to provide world-class customer service to your customers.

Your customers will see your brand through your teams, and everything that your teams say and do. Making sure your teams are 'on the same page' is part of your daily routine. Informing your teams how the business is performing on a daily basis, what is doing well and what is not doing well, is important to ensure everybody is focusing on the main issues that you wish to resolve and improve.

Implementing a great communication process will help your business achieve its goals:

- Make communication a priority across the whole business

- Hold a weekly team meeting where you discuss the previous week's performance, the learnings from this, the next week's highlights and any other important issues for your business in that week

- Ensure the main points from the meeting are relayed to the whole team shortly after the meeting

- Send out a report or have a daily morning meeting to cover any issues from the previous day and issues for the day ahead (for example, new products or promotions that may be happening). Keeping these meetings to five minutes a day maximum is more than enough

Develop loyalty in the team

Developing loyalty in the team will help keep the customers happy and satisfied – motivated and loyal team members will always give better customer service and be happy to go the extra mile for the customers. Loyal team members build consistency in the business and this helps to grow and develop the business for the customers.

Loyalty in the team helps to build rapport with the customers – when a customer sees the same person each time they visit your store, they feel more comfortable and are much more likely to shop with you again. This also significantly benefits the business, by allowing the team members to build up rapport with the customers who will then be able to gain more customer insights and more information about the customers' wants, needs and desires, allowing you to serve the customers better.

Loyalty is gained from working with the team and understanding the team. Setting up a strong culture and set of values, as described earlier, will help to make the team feel part of the business and help them live and breathe the values.

Loyalty from your team can be developed by:

- Regular and informative updates (weekly/daily meetings)
- A good induction process, so they feel part of the business from the first day
- Regular performance and development reviews – keeping them on track and developing
- Incentives and rewards – offer discounts, product trials and benefits for achieving targets

Create interest in your product and brand

Allowing and encouraging the team to interact with the products will grow loyalty and also allow for better selling of your products or service. If you have a team that knows and loves your products inside out, they are more likely to recommend the products sincerely to your customers – thus improving your sales.

Creating interest and excitement around the product is easy to implement at any stage of the product life cycle. During the planning phase you can use the team members as part of focus groups to discuss and debate the concepts and ideas you have for the current or new range. This can be very exciting for the team and make them feel fully part of the journey.

Once the product is launched you can allow the team to trial and test the product - taking the product home overnight, wearing the product or tasting the products are all easy to do and relatively inexpensive.

Discussing with the team the brand values and the products allows them to absorb the culture and start to become ambassadors for your brand - they will live and breathe the brand which will be seen by the customers and the people the team interacts with. This improves the selling ability of the team and makes it easier to interact with the customers.

You also need to ensure that during the trials, tests and focus groups, the team is finding out what the USP of your product is. Educating the team on why the product is different and what the benefits are for the customer will strengthen the selling ability of the team.

Creating interest in the brand and products can be achieved by:

- Focus group and design team meetings
- Product testing - at home, trials, testing, etc.
- Training the team on the benefits and USP of the products
- Allowing the team to live and breathe the brand

Remunerate the team to perform

Remuneration is often seen as the most important motivator to people in the workplace. Setting the correct pay and benefits level is a pre-requisite for a successful and happy team. Money on its own is not a motivator or de-motivator – it is a factor that is expected and as such you need to manage this carefully. We all want to earn more money, but we also know the value that is placed on the job roles we fulfil. Pay and benefits need to be in line with the values of the business – a high-end retailer must remunerate the staff according to the high expectations and perceptions of the customer segments.

Money is the basic level of remuneration and is expected by all employees. Where you can be creative and motivational is with the benefits and incentives. These include many areas such as: bonus, holidays, discounts, pensions, car benefits, health insurance, training, etc.

Making these attractive and competitive is important. You do not want to over-pay or be driving up salary inflation. A real problem we faced in the Shared Service Centre (SSC) in the Czech Republic was our ability to pay more; we could have started a salary increase across the whole region if we had set our salaries over the odds. Instead we offered better training and social activities to compete with the existing companies in the area, without increasing costs for the whole sector in the region.

How we set the remuneration package in the SSC

Providing good customer service is critical to successfully operating a business as large and complex as a multi-national retailer. As part of its drive to improve customer satisfaction, the business created an SSC for the finance function. The SSC was set up to provide financial services across several European countries and was located in Brno, Czech Republic. It had to service other companies within the group, across Europe, and had to provide the same customer service expected from its own retail stores.

The total rewards package needed to be flexible to allow all members of the team to feel motivated and appreciated. This was measured and offered to all the team so they could choose what suited their lifestyle. For example, some people liked extra holidays, whereas others preferred a higher pension contribution or bigger staff discounts.

A great way to motivate and reward the team was via social events. This could be offering the team a budget to hold an event every month, holding a company Christmas party, subsidising a weekend trip or holding a summer BBQ and Olympics. This not only rewarded the team, but built team camaraderie and bonding.

A good remuneration policy motivates and rewards the team:

- Benchmark the industry to ensure that you are competitive – look at outside companies or look at local jobs that are similar
- Offer flexible benefits – let the employees choose what they would like to take advantage of; for example offer extra training or hold social events
- Focus on non-cash incentives and rewards
- Use your products to provide benefits to both your team and your business

Remuneration benchmarking within your industry can be completed in a number of ways, with the starting place being:

- Local recruitment companies that deal with your local job market
- Your local government job centre, which will have information on local salaries and benefits
- Business support companies, such as your local Business Link and your local Chamber of Commerce
- Your local newspapers – have a look through the job adverts and you will get a great feel for the local salary and benefits offered by your competitors

Summary

- Develop a world-class customer-focused culture, throughout your entire business
- Recruit a high-performing team
- Live and breathe your values and culture
- Train the team to compete and be the best
- Communicate with the team
- Develop loyalty in the team
- Create interest in your product and brand
- Remunerate the team to perform

Chapter 15

Market Your Product And Brand

Having set up a great business with an amazing product range, a clearly-segmented customer base and a great team to deliver this, you need to then move into marketing your product and your brand. Marketing is the means by which you inform people that you and your products exist and takes many forms.

Marketing is often seen as advertising alone, through media such as TV adverts, newspaper adverts and online adverts, but marketing is much wider than this. Marketing looks at many different channels and forms, which all inform the customer that you and your products exist.

Forms of marketing

Advertising

Advertising is the first area that people consider when they talk about marketing. An advert is paid for and appears at exactly the time and place you want it to. You control its contents and its placement. The main advertising media are:

- Newspapers
- TV
- Radio
- Magazines
- Online display (e.g. banner adverts)
- Online paid marketing (e.g. Google Adwords and Facebook adverts)
- Outdoor

An advert can appear in a number of media as mentioned above, but must fulfil a number of basic criteria.

A good advertising campaign and theme will include:

- A clear message – an advertising campaign must have a purpose and this purpose should be clear and consistent. This is known as a 'call to action'.

For example, a retailer will give the message that you need to visit the store to see the new range or buy the latest offers in store

- A theme – a clear and coordinated theme is important, keeping all wording, imagery, messages and goals the same and for these to be seen as the same no matter what media channel is used

- Easy to understand – every advert must be simple and easy to understand. Each day we are bombarded with adverts and brand messages; to compete, yours must be simple and easy to understand in a few seconds

- Eye-catching – similar to the above point, we are all time-pressured and we need to see and understand the advert in a few seconds

- Coordinated and consistent – across all types of media and media channels, the messages and themes must be consistent for the customers to understand

- Call to action – the advert must have a call to action, i.e. there must be a call for the reader to do something; that could be visit the physical store, call a telephone number, visit the ecommerce website or watch a certain TV show

- Brand-driven – overall the brand values must be seen in the advertising. Adverts are normally the first contact a new customer will have with your business, so the adverts must portray the brand image that you have developed for your business

- A strapline – a common sentence that spans all the media and becomes well recognised. Large retailers use this extremely well – for example, 'Every Little Helps' and 'I'm Lovin' It' are well-known straplines that we see on all their adverts, be that TV, press or online. Not all companies use this, but it can be used to expand the brand understanding

A good marketing strategy will involve a comprehensive marketing campaign – this is where you co-ordinate a number of adverts, in a number of media and marketing channels. These must all 'feel' the same to the customers. Each separate type of media must portray the same message and image as the others; you should make sure that you develop a comprehensive theme that can span all types of media and channels you wish to use.

Advertising is the main form of marketing; other forms of marketing are discussed later, and include PR and sponsorship.

Marketing message

Tell the customer what you sell

In its most basic form, marketing is about telling the customer what you sell and why you exist. Marketing your product should ensure that the customer is aware that you exist and understands what products you sell – the aim of marketing should be to ensure that when people hear your brand they recognise that you sell a certain product range.

Over time, with brand marketing, you will expect the customers to be able to understand not only what you sell, but also know what your brand stands for and what they can expect when they shop with your business, i.e. they begin to understand your culture and your values.

When you are marketing to your customer, keep it simple. Make sure they know what you are selling, at what price (if this is part of the marketing message), where they can buy the product and why they should buy your product from your retail channels.

Making the customers aware of your products must be simple and efficient – a customer sees hundreds of marketing message each day, so a succinct and easy-to-remember marketing message is the key to success.

Tell the customer what the benefits of your product are

Once you have told your customer what you sell, you need to sell the benefits of your product versus your competition. You have already defined your customer segment and established what your customers want from your products; you now need to ensure that the customer knows what the benefits of your products and services are.

This is easy to forget and take for granted, but customers will not know what your product benefits are unless you tell them – building a brand and a business takes time, and you will always need to remind your customers what the benefits are of shopping with you.

Making the customer aware of your niche and your USP is key in your marketing messages. You have built your product and service for your customer segments and now you need to make sure that they are aware of what you have developed for them, and how this satisfies their wants, needs and desires.

To make sure your customers know about your products' and services' benefits you must:

- Communicate the benefits to them, clearly and consistently

- Make sure the communication is simple, but comprehensive

- Make sure you know your customers' communication preferences – find out what their preferred method is. Ask them via questionnaires, VIP events, asking your team etc.

- Communicate in the ways that they like to receive information e.g. mailings, emails, Tweets, telephone calls etc.

Develop a promotional strategy

Initially, your marketing strategy will involve your product and is very likely to talk about some type of promotional offer or event. It is important to develop a promotional strategy as early as possible and make sure this strategy is achievable.

A good promotional strategy will focus on the customer and what they will value the most in a promotion – some customer segments will value money off, others link-buys (to sell two products from different ranges that complement each other, such as a DVD player and a new release DVD), and others a VIP or exclusive event. Work with the customer segments and the brand values you have established and develop the promotional strategy to achieve these objectives.

A promotional strategy should cover:

- The types of promotions relevant to your customer segment
- Enhance and add value to any marketing campaign you are running
- Be of greater perceived value than the actual cost, e.g. a VIP event is perceived by customers of greater value than the actual cost of the event, or a free product with a purchase will be calculated at cost price and therefore be part of the whole strategic cost and benefits of a marketing campaign
- Set up the strategy at the beginning - you may decide to hold promotions at regular intervals or as and when you have good offers and product deals

Marketing online and offline

There are two main marketing channels - online and offline. We will look at these separately, but they should be used together, not separately. Understanding how your customer interacts with your business will help you choose the correct channel, and trialling different channels is a great way to find the perfect fit for your product and service.

Online marketing involves marketing your products and services in the intangible world of the internet, mobile phones, smartphones and using social media. Please see the online retail chapter for a greater understanding of the differing online marketing channels. In summary, the main areas are:

- SEO (search engine optimisation) - ensuring that your website is well-ranked in the search engines, that is, when someone types your product or service into Google, you want to be one of the first companies in the list that comes up, which encourages new customers to visit your website

- Affiliates -allowing another website to market your product to their customers in return for a commission

- PPC (pay per click) -advertising on search engines (like Google) and paying every time a person clicks on your links

- Direct adverts - setting up an advert directly on a website and paying for the placement of this advert

- Social media -using social media sites to make people aware of you and your product, and in some cases directly advertising

- Blogs -writing something related to your company and posting it online to create interest and awareness of your brand and your products

- Articles - writing articles on your subject of expertise and sending out on your website to build awareness and credibility

Offline marketing has been used for a long time and is also known as traditional marketing. This type of marketing is much more tangible than online marketing, and has been tried and tested over the years. Offline marketing is used less than it was a few years ago, but it is nevertheless a very important channel.

The main types of offline media:

- TV
- Radio
- Magazines
- Newspapers
- Journals
- Catalogues
- Samples
- Events
- Posters
- Leaflets

The main channels used for smaller retailers are normally newspapers, magazines, leaflets and local radio. Your choice of media should be dependent on what your customer segment uses. Understanding which media they use, and which media they value, will help you decide which form of media to use.

These types of media are more expensive than online and their results are much less measurable, but they are still the largest channels of media used, and customers still expect to buy your products after seeing adverts in these media channels. The number of types and the variety of these types means that there will be an excellent fit for your products and for your customers segments. Research, and some trial and error, will find which channels work the best for your business.

These channels have changed over time and will continue to change. Understanding the types of customers for each media channel is important, as these will have evolved over the last few years and will continue to do so over the next few years as customers wish to interact with your business in different ways.

Above all, the main goal is to make sure your advertising campaigns are co-ordinated and cross all the media channels your customers use, both online and offline.

Summary

- Understand the main forms of marketing
- Develop the basic requirements for an advert
- Tell the customer what you sell
- Tell the customer what the benefits of your product are – your USP
- Develop a promotional strategy
- Understand 'two track' marketing – to build the brand and to sell products
- Know the different marketing channels available to you
- Understand the importance of content online and offline

Chapter 16

Launch The Business And Sell, Sell, Sell

The sales process

Creating the best product in the world that is right for your customer, and they know it is available, is great, but one last step is missing – you must sell the product to the customer. Even though you have the perfect product for your customer and they know it exists, there is still some work to do in order to get them to hand over their hard-earned cash.

Selling is informing the customers about the benefits of your product

When a customer decides to buy a product, they have a need, desire or want they seek to fulfil. For example, when a customer decides to purchase a drill, they do not want to buy the drill; they want to hang a shelf on the wall, and therefore need to make a hole in the wall. Or a customer buys a pair of Armani jeans, not to keep warm but to express their fashion image and their personal status.

Understanding the benefits of your products means understanding what is important to your customer and the reason why they would enter your shop or visit your website. They visit your stores because they want a product that fulfils a need, desire or want they have.

Selling is enabling the customer to buy your product

Selling is the final stage to enabling the customer to buy your product at the right price, right time and with the right quality. Selling involves focusing on the benefits of your product – telling the customer why they should buy your product.

You already know what the customer wants, and you know what they value and like in life; you have set out your brand image and implemented a quality level – you must now sell your product to your customer.

Enabling the customer to buy the product involves informing them the:

- Product exists (via marketing)

- Product is available to take home or for delivery
- Benefits of the product (its USP)
- Pricing structure of the product range
- Added extras of the product (service plans, VIP clubs, link-buys etc.)

Selling techniques

There are many selling techniques that are available for retailers and many different proven strategies. Here, I will discuss the basic process and the simplest form of selling a product to a retail customer – this is mainly focused on a customer who is in a physical shop, but the principles can be adapted for an online store.

The basic principle in any selling transaction is to understand that the process is two-way – the customer has a need, want or desire and you have a product that meets that need, want or desire. Your team's role is to match the two in a simple and pleasant way, thus making the customer happy and making your business happy. This is called a 'win-win' scenario – when both parties are happy with the result and leave your business feeling satisfied.

The aim of the dialogue is to find out why the customer is in your retail outlet or has visited your website – what is their need, desire or want?

The two-way process in action:

- The first piece of information you need from the customer is why they are in your store – you can ask many questions to open this dialogue. Questions such as 'Good morning/afternoon/

evening, what brings you into our store today?'
This is an open question that allows the customer
to discuss with you straight away the problem or
reason why they need your product or service

- Finding out why they are in your store allows you
  to work out which benefits of your product will
  appeal to them and answer their question of what
  problem they are trying to solve with your product

- There are many reasons why customers visit your
  store, and capturing these trends over time and for
  each of your customer segments will be useful to
  train and develop your team and to plan further
  marketing and growth strategies

- Once the customer is engaged, make sure you
  'close the sale'; you must ensure you actually ask
  the person to buy the product and get them to pay
  or order the item. This is as easy as saying, 'You
  can pay for this over here', or 'Would you like this
  gift-wrapped?'

- Do not be afraid to close the sale – selling
  products is why you have the retail business in the
  first place

- Do not be afraid to up-sell and cross-sell.
  Up-selling is a process where you sell a higher
  value product to a customer based on the
  additional benefits the product offers and the
  needs of the customer

- Cross-selling is offering a complementary product
  that is beneficial for the customer to purchase. For

example, when you buy a DVD player you normally need a cable to attach it to your TV – without this, the DVD player is useless, and the customer will be disappointed

Selling online is slightly different, as you cannot engage in a direct two-way conversation as easily as you can within a physical store. An online sale is focused on the planning beforehand and understanding the needs of the customer before they visit your website. You then need to make sure your website easily answers the needs of your customers. Making your website simple and direct will mean the customer can find the product and buy it with ease.

Setting up a clearly-defined online product catalogue is important to enable the customer to find the products they need, based on their reason for visiting your store. Over time you can adapt the website to answer questions for the customers, for example: 'Having problems putting up your shelf? Click here to see our latest range of drills'.

Using a checkout that is simple and intuitive is important to close the sale. A one-page or integrated checkout is the most successful, which allows quick access of details and the ability to check out in one click.

At the checkout you can also cross-sell and up-sell. Analysing your customers' purchases will allow you to link products that you know customers will see as complementary to their purchase or needed with their purchase.

Make sure the sales process is in line with your brand values

Understanding your customer segments and their values is useful for developing your selling process. You must ensure that your sales process reflects the values of the brand and that of your customers. You should not over-sell your products, and neither should you under-sell your products – both of these will cause customer service issues and complaints.

We have all experienced the hardcore selling tactics – known historically in the car sales industry, where it was common for them to use any tactics possible to get you to buy a used car. This approach is still used in some high-pressure sales channels, but in the main these are not common in retailers and in most cases would cause a negative result from the customer.

The selling process should be in line with your values and

- Demonstrate an understanding of how your customer likes to shop and therefore how they would like to be treated when they interact with your business. A high fashion store will have a very attentive service and sales process, whereas a local newsagent will be a quick and pleasant interaction

- Acknowledge the customers, and make sure they know that you and your team are there for them, is important for all sales opportunities – u greet all your customers and apply the right amount of sales pressure your team feels necessary in order to fulfil the customer's need, and gain the important closed sale

Launching your business and PR

When you set up the business, renew or refresh the business or develop a new product range, you need to plan a launch campaign and PR strategy to capitalise on the opportunity to gain 'free PR' and make sure you get off to the best start you possibly can.

PR (public relations) is different from advertising and is the process by which you approach the press (TV, radio, newspapers, magazines, bloggers, articles etc.) to write an article about your new product or store.

Good PR is being able to deliver an interesting story to the readers of the media – all journalists need interesting stories to engage their readers on a regular basis, so any great news story is beneficial to them and their readers.

It is important to make sure there is a story – opening a new store or launching a new product range is an OK story, but it needs some interest and relevance to the receivers of the press. Thinking about the details of the story is vital: the point of interest could be, for example:

- A local focus: 'Local store opens and employs 10 people from the local community'
- A new and intriguing focus: 'Retailer launches brand new shirts that eliminate sweat patches'
- A good news story: 'Retailer launches new product range that is 50% less wasteful'

Developing an interesting story is a simple process:

- Draft a few 'news' stories about the launch

- Review the PR channels and target the ones that suit your launch campaign
- Tailor the articles for the relevant readers/ consumers of the articles – make it relevant to the end readers
- Write the article and make it easy for the journalist to use and understand – they have very little time and many articles to read each day
- Develop a plan and co-ordinate the whole process. Be aware that PR is not controlled, and you can only give the best shot at getting into the relevant press you would like it in
- Collate all the PR and use that in your adverts – PR builds credibility and is important for brand building

The final part of the launch is to hold some form of launch event – making sure that a large number of people know you have launched is important to give your business the best start possible. Plan an event and invite the relevant people, e.g. for a local store opening, invite the local dignitaries, the local press and some of the local community; for a new ecommerce website, launch on the relevant blogs and news spaces, as well as social media platforms.

The most successful PR campaign is planned and thought out – some of the PR will not be used or will not work, but you must plan a number of different PR items and a few of them will give you the desired effect.

Social media and PR

The boundary between social media and PR has blurred significantly and we are now able to write our own PR stories and share them for free across blogs and social media networks.

Gone are the days when you had to contact a PR agency, who would charge you to write your story and distribute it. You now have the power. Does this mean that there is no need for a PR agency? I believe there is a place for a PR agency, but they must understand and be experts in social media as well as traditional PR.

There are two major benefits of using a PR company:

- They have an understanding of the different styles of writing that work for certain types of media. They understand and use the best techniques for online and offline PR, which is something that you will not have expert knowledge of

- They have a 'black book' of contacts. With social media it is significantly easier to contact and interact with thought leaders and influencers. This does take time, but it is completely possible to do this yourself. Where a PR expert can add value is by having a list of contacts, both online and offline, who they can contact and market your business and your book to. Personal contact and personal connection is still the way that the best business deals are done

Overall, I believe that a good PR expert, who is aware and uses social media, can be an asset to your shop online and offline. They can offer the outside view on your business, and can offer the expert advice and knowledge when you need it.

Chapter 21, the online retail case study, explains in depth the process we used to market FreshMax Shirts and promote our ecommerce business.

Summary

- The selling process is about informing the customers of the benefits (USP) of your product
- Selling is enabling the customer to buy your product
- Understand selling techniques
- Make sure the sales process is in line with your brand values
- PR - launching your business (new, refreshed or a new product range)

Chapter 17

Customer Service Is Everything

Welcome to the customer service chapter; this is only a small chapter as the whole book centres around the customer. This chapter looks at specific customer service best practice that is not part of the other steps in the journey.

Customers are the key to the success of your business; without them you do not exist and without them you cannot be successful. Making the customer the heart of your business is the only way to achieve retail excellence. The positive effect of a total customer focus is a happy customer, which in turn makes your teams happy, which makes you happy and also makes your business profitable in the process.

Think customer – everybody is a customer

Every part of the business must 'think customer' – you only exist to service the customer and therefore every part of the business must understand how their actions affect the ultimate customer. Thinking customer involves immersing the whole business in your customer's lifestyle and how your customer likes to live and shop.

A world-class customer service culture is developed by ensuring all the team understand not only how they affect the end customer, but how they are also a customer and everybody they interact with is part of the customer's journey.

Every team in your business has a customer and is a customer; a customer in this case can be described as anybody you interact with in your daily routine. The easiest way to think of this is to look at, and treat, everybody you interact with as if they were the ultimate end customer who buys your products. Greet them, chat with them, understand them and then deliver what they need from you. This is applicable to everybody in the business, no matter what their responsibilities are.

Trained and customer-focused teams

A happy, trained and motivated team will always offer the best customer service they possibly can – they are trained and motivated to do so. Training your team starts at the interview, where you must ensure you recruit customer-minded and customer-focused team members. Once you have recruited these you must train them on who the customers are and what they value.

Valued team members not only provide good customer service, they also motivate each other to keep improving and delivering for your business.

Keep the customers loyal

Once you have established a relationship with your customer you must maintain this relationship. A loyal customer is of great value to your business, because they know you, like you and shop with you. When you have loyal customers, you can easily email or call them with your latest offers or new product ranges to enable more sales and gain more information about your customers.

Loyal customers are also the best sales team you will ever have – a happy loyal customer will tell all their friends about your products, and their personal recommendation is not only free, it also means more to the potential customer than any advertising and marketing campaigns that you may run.

For an online business, the loyal customer is even more important due to the use of social media – imagine your customer tweeting about your great store experience or the great product they have just bought. This can be read by millions of people and help drive traffic to your website and customers visiting your physical store.

To keep a loyal customer, you need to give them what they require from your business; you will know this from understanding your customer and developing your products for them. You need to be consistent in your execution within your business and ensure happy customers leave your business every time.

Making your customers feel special can be achieved by:

- Regular updates on what's hot and what's new
- Interesting stories about the business and the team
- Regular incentives and special offers
- VIP events and offers
- Talking to them and listening to their feedback

Simple returns and exchanges

This area of customer service is easy to forget during the journey, but is an area that must be made simple and efficient - especially with an online store. Customers expect to have the ability to change their mind and change their products as easily and simply as possible. Poor returns and exchanges will prevent customers from shopping with you in the first place. In the current retail world, the customers' expectation is that they are able to exchange a product if they do not like it - a no quibble and no fuss exchange or return.

A good returns and exchanges process involves implementing:

- A clear returns and exchanges policy stating how long the customers have to return the items, what condition, where to send them, etc.

- Trained teams that know how to deal with the returns and exchanges – make sure all your team know how the returns and exchanges process works to ensure great customer service
- A process for disposing of product or reselling the returned product
- A way for the customers to send the products back easily – free returns labels and some companies are now offering a returns service from a local 'collection point'

Test the customer service

A well-trained, customer-service-focused team will be able to service your customers every day in a consistent and positive way, but sometimes team members' attention will slip and you need to ensure that consistency is applied all the time.

Using test shoppers and mystery shoppers is a big benefit to any serious retailer; all the large retailers carry out regular tests and mystery shops to ensure the processes and training procedures are correct and work for customers.

When you carry out a test or mystery shop, ensure all the feedback is captured and passed on to the team members involved, to help improve their way of working. You can also use the total data to address any company training issues or process issues that may have been exposed.

Customer feedback is key to your future success

Gathering as much customer feedback and opinions as possible will help you grow and develop your business successfully. Keeping close to your customers enables you to find out what works, what does not work and what needs to change.

Implemented in a positive way, customer feedback can drive your future growth and planning decisions, as the customer can tell you what they want from your brand and your business.

Using all the possible channels to gather this data is important and you should utilise as many as possible:

- Transactional data
- Email data
- Your teams' interactions
- Questionnaires
- Sales data
- VIP events
- Surveys
- Blogs and social media monitoring
- Incentives and promotional events

Gathering this data will help you throughout the journey and is mentioned in most sections of this handbook – it is an important part of understanding your customer.

Think world-class customer service

A total understanding of your customer is the best way to achieve your potential in retail.

How do you develop a total understanding of your customers?

- Develop a totally customer-focused culture
- Remember: everybody you and your teams interact with is a customer
- Train your teams on customer service and customer interactions
- Inform your teams of the different customer segments you target, why you target these and what they 'look' like
- Focus your teams on interacting with the customers, let the teams spend time with the customers so they can be your 'eyes and ears' on behalf of the customers
- Keep your customers happy and loyal – a loyal customer is a 'free' sales channel
- Test the customer experience
- Gain as much customer feedback as you can – this can help you develop more and more profitable sales, products and ranges

Social media customer service

The digital world has embraced social media as part of the new connected world we live in. This has led to a significant increase in the use of social media for customer service.

Social media in all its form, is simple and easy to use with the customer having the power to tweet or post bad reviews and feedback. As mentioned in the principles section, any retailer and brand must embrace social media and ensure they respond to their customer as quickly and thoroughly as they can.

Some of the world's leading brands look at social media customer service as a profit centre. They allocate time and resources to 'listen' to the customers and potential customers. This listening enables them to react to issues quickly and to find out what people are discussing and the wants, needs and desires they have.

Retailing is simple, you sell what the customers want, need and desire – social media listening allows you to find out some of these requirements and enables you to inform your customers of the products you have that can help them.

Bad social media customer service will be seen by all current and future customers. This is a permanent reminder that your product and service was bad and no response is unforgivable.

Summary

- Think customer – everybody is a customer
- Develop trained and customer-focused teams
- Keep the customers loyal
- Enable simple returns and exchanges
- Test the customer service
- Customer feedback is key to your future success
- Think world-class customer service
- Establish good quality social media customer service

Chapter 18

Merchandise And Manage Your Stock

Making sure your stock is correct for your target market helps you deliver world-class customer service - your customers are ultimately visiting your store to buy your stock. You need to ensure that everything is perfect, with the right stock, in the right place, at the right price for your customer segments that your business targets.

Stock is extremely valuable and should be viewed and treated as if it were cash. Stock has two financial values: the first is the stock value, which is the price for which you bought the stock; the second is the retail value which is the price for which you intend to sell the stock.

The difference between the two is the margin. This could be very large or small depending on whether you are in a high-value or low-value business. The size of the margin is linked to the way you manage your costs and will make you a profit or loss.

The right stock

Understanding what is the right stock and sourcing this at the right price is key to being able to satisfy your customer needs. Your customer segments will inform you what your product range should be, and from that range you can decide what the exact product mix should look like. Research and test market all the variants possible: colours, sizes, styles, brands, options etc. and make sure the products are complementary to each other and fit well as a range in the customers' eyes.

Buying the right stock will come from your sourcing strategy and will be redefined at this stage as you begin to order and forecast what quantities you need to buy in order to meet the customer demand.

The best initial stock level

Deciding on the correct stock level at the beginning is difficult; you have no history and your products, service and brand combination is unique. Spending time planning the first orders is important, not only because it is a big cash investment, but also due to this being the first range and you need to ensure full availability during your opening period.

You will gain an understanding of your customers' buying patterns over the first few weeks, so your initial plan should be to satisfy a reasonable forecast of what you will sell before your second delivery of products will arrive. As part of your sourcing strategy you will have decided on the distribution plan and this will need to be tested during your first few trading weeks.

The best initial stock level means you need to forecast your sales until your second delivery and ensure you have enough stock for full availability during the initial days of trading. Once you have been trading a few days, out of stocks are less important as you start to understand your customers' shopping patterns – it is important to keep the stock levels tight as you learn how your customers shop and in what quantities they buy your products.

You will over- or under-forecast some products and maybe even some ranges – this is to be expected. Nobody can ever forecast the exact requirements of the customers. Make sure you have put in place a process to deal with under- and over-stocks – under-stocks will need a good customer service response, e.g. 'We can order the product' or 'We have this product, which is similar' and over-stocks must be dealt with quickly via markdowns and promotions.

Manage your continuing stock levels

Maintaining a good level of stock is a hard task to achieve in the first few months of trading. Stock management is affected by many outside influences that, in the main, you do not control. Knowing your optimum stock level for your business at the start is based on your best guess. The more planning you have done and the more time you have spent with your customers and team, the more reliable your forecasts will be.

When you plan your sourcing strategy you will have looked at how you will distribute and warehouse your products. This plays a role in deciding on your continuing stock levels.

If you can negotiate more regular deliveries, you will need to hold less stock - thus being cheaper and easier to manage, but you may run out of stock more often, which could lead to poor customer service. You need to plan where you think your balance is between the two and refine it over time.

Forecasting the initial stock needs to be an educated guess using the facts and information you are currently aware of. You could use the following to build up your forecasts:

- Any previous history
- Other shops'/businesses' data and trends
- Data and forecasts from your suppliers
- Customer feedback
- Team feedback
- Sales plans you have in place
- Marketing, promotions and PR you are planning

Develop a commercial/buying plan

All these forecasts should be used to start a commercial plan. A commercial or buying plan is a forecast of what you need to buy in order to fulfil your expected sales. You already have a marketing and promotional plan in place; a commercial plan should be implemented to ensure that you buy enough products to fulfil your sales and marketing plans.

Once you have a few weeks' sales history, you can set up your stock replenishment process. This is a process by which you re-order or review your stock levels when you are nearing the end of a product's current stock holding.

Feeding your sales data into your commercial planning process enables you to automate the process based on rules. For your main stock range, you could set minimum levels at which you order stock. For example, you may have a supply chain that takes four weeks from order and you know you sell 100 items a week. When you get to 450 items you should re-order; this is because you currently sell 100 items a week and delivery takes four weeks, hence you will have 50 items left when the new delivery arrives.

This process can be put in place for all your products at an individual product level, but should be reviewed often as sales patterns change.

Cost price negotiations

Agreeing a cost price on every product is a trade-off or balance between three competing areas:

- Price – the price you pay for the product

- Payment terms –the agreed length of time you have to pay the supplier for your product
- Quantity –the amount or level of stock you wish to buy

Achieving a balance in cost price

The balance to be achieved between these three areas depends on your own business's needs and resources:

- Price – do you have the cash to invest in stock? A bank loan can be agreed and the stock used as a guarantee if need be.

- Payment terms – can you afford to pay your suppliers sooner or later? You can always 'factor' these invoices – this means that a bank or finance company pays the supplier sooner rather than later and you pay them at a later date.

- Quantity – do you have enough room to store a large amount of stock?

The trade-off should look at how much you are willing to pay for a product and how long you wish the repayment period to be.

For example, I have a small stock room and a low cash holding. I would be best to negotiate a slightly higher cost price, but a longer payment period, to ensure I sold the products before I paid the supplier, but I also make a good gross profit.

Using a commercial plan and modelling tools, you can easily calculate the best cost price to agree, the payment period and quantity.

How much to order

A minimum order level and also a minimum order quantity should be calculated. Once your products reach the minimum stock level, you need to calculate how many to order – this can be a rule, based on stock levels required and warehousing capacity. For example, you could re-order at 450 stock level and you re-order for four weeks (100 items sold per week), therefore ordering another 400 items.

Over time you can make many rules to calculate these figures to ensure you have the optimum stock level to meet the customers' needs and manage your cash and risk levels. If you do not want to have this level of sophistication, you can buy on a regular basis, i.e. every month, and each time you order have a look at what you sold the previous period and what you forecast to sell in the next period. Make sure you include any promotions and marketing campaigns you may have planned.

The commercial planning process looks at the following areas:

- An understanding of your product range
- A forecast (by individual product) of what you think you will sell in a set period of time
- An understanding of your marketing, PR, launch and promotional strategy will drive part of the forecast
- An understanding of the desired stock levels
- A re-order process to calculate how many to order and how often

- An understanding of sourcing and distribution
- A view of the markdown process
- A plan to remove poorly-performing stock

Once you have the initial plan you can start to use this plan as a basis for the future. Add the actual sales figures to the forecast plan and start to track any trends that are appearing; these will help build you better forecasts in the future.

The main points to take into account in a commercial and buying strategy:

- Buy frequently - negotiate a deal on long delivery products and 'call off' the stock at regular intervals
- Manage the stock accurately and carry out stock takes regularly - you need to know your stock is accurate so you can forecast future orders and fulfil your customers' needs
- Act on slow sellers - do not be afraid to mark down products as soon as you realise they are not selling - clearing out slow sellers not only frees up cash but allows you to replace the products with new products the customers want and desire
- Check the commercial plans versus the marketing and promotional strategies - does it look like you have enough stock to fulfil the plans? Are you buying the correct products for the plans and promotions?
- Do not be over-optimistic - we all like to be positive and bullish, but you must balance a big forecast and order against the stock not selling and you making a loss on all your products. It is

better to sell out in the first few weeks rather than run out of cash and go bankrupt because you are not selling all the stock you bought

Stock is cash

Cash is the most important financial measure in a business. Businesses fail due to lack of cash, not due to lack of profits. After fixed assets such as the building and fixtures, stock is likely to be the biggest investment a retailer makes and, ongoing, one of the biggest costs in the business. Planning your stock is critical to the company's financial health and a wrong decision could ultimately bankrupt the retailer.

Managing the buying price (the price you pay for your products) is important to make sure you will make a profit, but you also need to manage the stock turns (the number of times you sell the products each year) and the stock holding. Both factors affect cash and product availability, and ultimately will affect the customers' experience.

A faster stock turn with more frequent deliveries is the best option – this frees up cash and deals with poorly-performing products quickly. New ranges appear often and the customers are kept excited and enticed by your constantly-changing product range that is targeted to them.

You will often have a large proportion of core products that you always sell, and a smaller proportion of new and exciting stock that you buy in smaller quantities and sell to your loyal customers.

Good stock management involves:

- Good commercial plans that are linked to the marketing plans and based on sound financial forecasts
- A defined product range
- A good supply chain and warehousing strategy
- Thorough checks of the delivery quantities
- Regular and thorough stock checks
- Quick action on poor sellers and markdowns
- Fast stock turns
- Exciting new products
- Management of theft and loss – all retailers suffer from products going missing
- Management shrinkage – all retailers suffer from products being damaged
- Good returns and exchanges management
- Special care of high value stock

Develop a markdown strategy

A markdown strategy is a plan of how you will deal with stock that is not selling as well as you had planned. All ranges will have some products that do not meet the customers' needs and will not sell as well as the rest of the range. You must act on these products quickly – remember that stock is cash and stock not selling is destroying the value of that cash.

To develop a markdown strategy, you need to go back to the values of the brand and define what types of markdowns and promotions you wish to operate.

There are many options available, but you would normally use:

- Percentage reduction
- Fixed reduction
- 'Buy one get one free'
- Multibuys, e.g., 3 for 2 or buy this product and get another half price
- Money off a following visit or purchase

Setting a formal markdown process is important to manage profits, minimise losses and keep the stock moving. An example of a markdown strategy for a fashion store: one month after launch of the range, products that have more than 75% of the average stock level for that range should be discounted 10%; one month later that should be 20%, etc.

Developing a markdown strategy from the beginning of your journey will enable you to clearly implement the rules of markdowns as part of your normal operating business.

Reviewing your stock levels and your markdown discounts should be fully calculated and some products you will sell at a loss. This is normal practice in retail; the key is to make sure you sell more products at a higher margin and profit than you sell at a loss.

Merchandise to sell

Buying the right stock for your brand and image needs to be thought of when you plan the merchandising of your range. Merchandising describes the methods you use which contribute to the sale of your products. In a physical store, merchandising refers to the product range available and the display of your products in such a way that it stimulates interest and entices customers to buy your products. The same rules apply online – setting out your homepage and catalogue structure is important to understand for good customer service.

When you plan your range, you must think about how the products will look to the customer, and how easily the customer will be able to find the products they need. Arranging your product range is very important; your customers need to be able to easily find the products you sell and identify where the products are located in the store or online.

The main element to merchandising is the way you display and position your products. Making your products look the best they possibly can and be as 'in situ' as possible is important. Making your products look 'in situ' is achieved by setting up a store that is similar to where the product will be used by your customers. For example, in fashion stores the use of mannequins is the main way of displaying products in situ, and in a cooking products store laying out products on tables etc. will help the customer find the products they wish to purchase.

You can use merchandising principles to differentiate to your customer segments. We all know fashion stores are split into ladies' and men's sections, and then casual and formal, but you could also set up 'lifestyle' sections (use the imagery from your customer segmentation process) and you could then set up a mannequin that is dressed in a total 'lifestyle' look, e.g. sporty or dinner date etc. Merchandising all the products physically nearby will help the customer imagine what it would look and feel like to own all your product range.

Merchandising accessories and linked products near to your core products is very important. For a linked or secondary product, you must make it simple for the customer to buy the product. Retailers normally do this either by putting the secondary products next to the core merchandise, for example, belts near trousers, batteries near toys, cables near DVD players; or putting them by the tills (this is very common in supermarkets).

On the ecommerce store you can easily purchase programmes that show related or linked products when the customer adds products to the basket or when they are checking out.

Segment your product range for the customers

Segmentation should be customer-focused, not your own internal buying plans. This is very important and a very common trap that retailers fall into. For buying and merchandising purposes, it is easier to follow your product development plan and be internal looking. If you have followed this book and set your product range up for the customer segments, you will already be able to merchandise for the customers.

A great example of non-customer-focused segmentation is in the electricals retailing industry. The standard names for the categories are: brown, white and grey goods – what are they? As a customer, do you know (or care) what a white good is? The truth is you do care, as you want to buy a washing machine; you just need to know which area the product is in. You would find a washing machine in the kitchen appliances section. In a customer's view (in store and online) these will be categorised as: TVs, Computing, Large Appliances, and Kitchen Appliances etc. - categories that a customer understands and would look for in a shop.

Merchandising online

Different skills are needed to merchandise your products online. In store you are dealing with a large physical space where the customers can follow signs and instructions to find the products they are looking for.

Online this is not the case. A customer can only find a limited amount of information and you need to provide them information on every different size of screen and device - in some cases you have to merchandise a 5″ screen.

The way to merchandise online is driven by your understanding of the customer journey and how your customers search to find your products. If your customers know the product they want, they will type the product name into a search engine and they will find what they are looking for.

If they are browsing, they need to follow a logical journey to find the information and options available for the want, need or desire they are trying to fulfil.

Understand your customers' journeys and think about how you can merchandise these journeys on a 5″ screen - it takes a lot of research and planning to deliver great online merchandising.

Summary

- Find the right stock and the best initial stock level
- Develop a commercial/buying plan
- Manage your continuing stock levels
- Negotiate prices in line with your business's needs and resources
- Regulate your cash flow through good stock management
- Develop a markdown strategy
- Merchandise to sell
- Segment your product range for the customers
- Understand online merchandising

Chapter 19

Manage Your Information And Finance

Once your business is up and running, you will have vast amounts of information which is valuable to your business, if you manage it correctly. Using real data that is from the trading of the business and from your customers can help improve and develop many parts of your business.

Understanding your finances and managing them are vital for a successful and profitable business. Knowing where your money comes from and goes to is something you should understand on a regular basis - even daily for sales and cash. Remember: you must manage cash correctly - 'Cash is King' and without cash your business will fail.

Know and understand your profit and loss account

Your profit and loss account (P&L) is the place to find out where your money comes from and where it goes to. It starts with the money coming in (sales revenue), it takes off the cost of those sales (cost of goods sold) to give you the profit from your product buying (gross margin). Once you have your gross margin you take off all your other costs and you are left with your profit (or loss).

P&Ls should be reviewed on a weekly or monthly basis - in the beginning, managing your P&L daily is important to make sure you know where you are spending your cash. Understanding the P&L allows you to make business decisions based on real facts within your business. Over time you will need to make positive and negative decisions, and these will all have an effect on the P&L; understanding that impact before you make a decision is very important.

The easiest way to get to know your P&L is by looking at it regularly; starting with sales which you can review every day.

Plan, forecast and budget your finances

It is important to start planning what the costs and revenue impacts are to your business of all the previous plans that you have been developing on this journey. Once you have an understanding of your product, commercial plan and an understanding of your marketing and sales plan, you can then put together a budget or forecast that predicts what you plan to sell each week and what the cost of those sales will be.

With the rest of the plans you have looked at, you will then be able to forecast the costs within the business. These can then be measured to ensure you are on track and the business is performing as you wish it to.

A BASIC PROFIT AND LOSS FORMAT
(BUDGET, FORECAST OR ACTUAL)

Budget/ Forecast/Actual	Period 1	Period 2	Period 3
Sales revenue			
Cost of goods			
Gross margin			
Costs: Staff Rent/Rates Marketing/ Advertising Store overheads Delivery/Logistics Finance/Admin			
Profit before Tax			

This format can be used for different periods (i.e. weeks, months, years) and different types (i.e. actual, budget, forecast). All formats should remain consistent and all items should be calculated in the same way; this will enable comparisons and trends to be analysed.

'Cash is King'

The management of cash will make or break a business – businesses fail due to lack of cash, not lack of profits; therefore, managing the cash and the bank account is extremely important.

The retail industry is a great 'cash' industry that most industries would be jealous of, because of its ability to manage to a positive cash flow situation. This means that as a retailer (in certain sectors) you can retail products that are bought by the customer before you have paid the supplier – this is called positive cash flow, as you will have the money in the bank from the customer before you pay for the products you just sold. Since the financial crisis this has been much harder to achieve, but striving to achieve a positive cash flow is a great target.

The way to manage to a positive cash flow situation is to set up your suppliers' payment terms for a longer period than you need to sell the item; for example, if you negotiate payment terms of 60 days with your supplier and you sell the product to your customer for cash on day 30, you will have 30 days left before you pay your supplier. Of course, to make this happen you need to have a trading history, a good credit record and be able to sell the majority of your stock sooner than you pay the supplier.

Whichever method you use to manage your supplier relationships and customer relationships, you need to manage cash on a daily basis. A simple reconciliation each day of your sales revenues and your costs can easily ensure you know where you are with your finances.

CASH FLOW STATEMENT

Budget/ Forecast/ Actual	Period 1	Period 2	Period 3
Balance Brought Forward	£5,000	£10,000	£8,000
Sales Revenue (Cleared)	£10,000	£10,000	£10,000
Cost of Goods		£10,000	
Costs:			
Staff		£2,000	
Rent/Rates	£5,000		
Marketing/Advertising			£5,000
Store Overheads			
Delivery/Logistics			£2,000
Finance/Admin			
Balance Carried Forward	£10,000	£8,000	£11,000

In this example cash flow, we started the period with £5,000 in cash in the bank and made cash sales of £10,000. We then paid the rent and ended the period at £10,000 cash in the bank. This was then rolled forward to the next period and we then spent £2,000 on staff expenses leaving £8,000 in the bank.

As you can see, this simple model will ensure you can monitor and manage your cash. At the end of any period you should be able to reconcile the balance carried forward figure easily to your bank balance and any borrowings you may have.

Planning your cash flow from day one will help you understand your peaks and troughs with regard to cash. Most retailers have seasonal peaks and, in the main, this happens at Christmas (for example an electrical retailer will make 60% of their profit and sales in the three months from November to January). Managing cash during the quiet periods could be challenging, as there will be times of the year when sales are very low, but you still have to pay monthly bills etc. Planning this in advance will allow you to approach your bank and ask for a flexible loan or an overdraft - most retailers will use flexible financing through the quieter sales periods.

Customers and debtors

A debtor is an entity that owes your business money for services or products and in the main they will be your customers.

Managing customer payments into the business depends on the type of product you offer and can involve:

- Cash
- Credit cards
- Invoicing
- Payment plans (i.e. hire purchase agreements or store cards)
- Deposits
- Loans over a long term

The aim of the best cash flow policy is to get the cash as quickly as possible into your business, and the obvious quickest way to achieve that is to ask the customers to pay with cash. Unfortunately, this is not a possibility in most retailers today.

Credit cards are the normal method of payment in most retailers now, and this will deposit the cash into your bank account in three to ten working days. Most people expect this instantly, but this is not the case and you need to manage the payment terms to reflect the number of days before the real cash clears your bank account as cash.

Invoicing is used for larger orders and more business-related sales. This is where you invoice the customer on the day of purchase and allow them 15, 30 or more days to pay. With invoicing it is important to manage the debtors (the business or person that owes you the money) and make sure that you chase the invoices if they have not been paid on time. It is also worth credit checking the customers and setting each customer a credit limit, so that you manage the risk of any bad debt and non-payment of your invoices.

If you offer instalments, again you need a strong process to manage the payments and ensure that you receive all the payments due to you, and on time. Longer term loans and credit agreements can be outsourced to a financing company, which will take the risk away from your business and take a small commission for their risk and taking on the debt.

Suppliers and creditors

A creditor is an entity to which you owe money – the main creditor for a retailer will be your suppliers, but you will also owe money to a number of other parties, such as landlords, service providers and the tax man.

Managing your suppliers is an important part of managing your profitability and your cash flow. When you are negotiating the buying price for the product you must also agree the payment terms; in cash flow terms, the longer the payment terms the better, but there is a balance between a good product cost and a good payment term.

Using the cash flow planner and making sure you know when your customers' cash clears will help you decide what the best payment term plan is for your business and what plan you need to agree with your suppliers.

In summary, to manage your cash efficiently you need to:

- Plan and forecast the cash flow
- Negotiate payment terms with your suppliers
- Ensure you collect the cash from your customers
- Consider staggered payments both into and out of your business
- Negotiate flexible financing with your banks

Analysis identifies trends and aids good decision-making with regards to your cash flow and finances.

Analyse your information – KPIs

Analysis is best described as 'making sense of information and data'. In your business you will have a lot of information and data – from sales, customers, products, adverts, etc. – and all this data is useful to you and your business. As long as you can understand what the data is telling you, you will be able to act on this information.

Finding out what all the information and data means is where you start to do analysis. Analysis needs to be simple and customer-focused; you are looking for trends and information that will improve your business, which means the improvements you need to make to enable your customer to be satisfied.

The main analysis any retailer will look at will be the sales and the margins. You need to understand what this is telling you: where you are selling products, what products are selling and what products are not selling. You also need to understand what products are making you a good margin and what are making poor margins, and act on this analysis.

A list of the main areas to analyse is below (this is just a start; in your business there will be many more things that you can analyse to help improve your business):

- Sales
  - What products are selling
  - What products are not selling
  - How many products are selling
  - What customer segments are buying
  - Which channels are products selling in
  - What times of the day and which days do products sell
- Margins
  - What each product margin is
  - How much you are marking down/discounting products
  - Which customer segments are better margin contributors

- Costs
  - ▲ Staffing
  - ▲ Logistics and Delivery
  - ▲ Marketing
  - ▲ Promotions
  - ▲ Overheads

Analysis of all these areas will help to identify trends and these are important for decision making. For example, if you analyse sales by customer segment, you may find that one segment is continually buying lower margin products; you can then investigate why this is happening and work out a strategy to convert these customers to higher margin products.

Once you have identified a trend, and you have investigated the reasons for that trend, you must act and develop a strategy to improve or develop this trend. Ongoing analysis and building up an understanding of the trends and drivers within your business will help you buy better products, reduce costs and make a healthy profit.

Lots of information and analysis is great, but you need to act on this information and make sure you put plans in place to achieve the improvements desired. Many businesses make the mistake of not acting on the analysis and end up in a worse situation because of this - make sure you make a decision and change things based on the analysis.

Insight and actions

You must use all the information you have for analysis to make insights and then take actions. Insight is the drawing of conclusions and themes from the analysis to inform a decision that you can make.

Once you make this decision you can then implement the change and follow the changes to see what happens next. You will then analyse the results and continue the cycle.

KPIs - Key Performance Indicators

We hear lots of talk about KPIs and I wonder how many of these are actual KPIs - in most companies I have interacted with, they have a large number of KPIs and I always challenge this - the first word is 'key', which means important. If this is the case, how can you have so many KPI's?

Key is key - so make sure you only measure a few key PIs - the rest are more detailed PIs. I have also discussed online KPIs in detail in Chapter 6.

Information is power

The more information you have in your business, the more likely you will be able to make sound decisions, based on good analysis and trends. Examples of collecting as much information as possible have been shown all the way through your journey and continuing to collect data is a good practice to get into.

Once you have all the information for your analysis, as described earlier, you can then make informed and sound decisions to develop and improve your strategy. Collecting raw data from your sales and systems is a great process to implement, but you also need to collect customer data and more subjective data – this is the data that comes from your teams and customers via everyday interactions, events and questionnaires.

Building up a stronger picture and understanding of your customer will allow you to buy better products and market your business better to achieve the satisfaction of your customers' wants, needs and desires.

Managing the information in your businesses requires specialist skills, which you may need to outsource or recruit into the business. Recruit for or focus the analyst on:

- Understanding and analysing the raw sales and financial data
- Establishing trends in the figures
- Cross-referencing and sense-checking the data. Does it look reasonable? Is it telling us some useful information?
- Understand the information deeper – data will show trends that happen, but you need to understand why this is happening. You do this by looking at customer data and feedback, discussing with your teams and asking the relevant people their opinions and views
- Use the information to make decisions – make sure the information and analysis is robust enough to enable you to make decisions and plan new strategies

Summary

- Know and understand your profit and loss account
- Plan, forecast and budget your finances
- Keep track of your cash
- Manage your customers and debtors
- Manage your suppliers and creditors
- Analyse your information
- Identify the important key metrics for your business

Chapter 20

Build A Strong Foundation For Growth

Setting up any business or growing a business is extremely challenging in any market. Retail is a massively competitive market, but is full of many opportunities that have been missed by the larger retailers or missed by the current smaller retailer base.

A new retailer, or an existing retailer wishing to improve their business, should focus on the customer and making sure they achieve what the customer wants; if they do that they will be successful. To build a sustainable and successful business longer term, you must build a strong foundation for the future potential of your business.

Ensure everything you set up and put in place is capable of supporting your business in the long term as you grow and develop.

We all know that the best-built houses are built with deep and strong foundations – the type of houses that were built hundreds of years ago and are still as strong today. It is hard to build a strong foundation, because it feels like you are digging down and not achieving anything, but this is exactly how successful retailers operate. They spend more time analysing, planning and building than they do operating; once they start daily operations, the team and the business runs itself (with a trained team in place) and the owners can focus on building the next set of strategies because they know the foundations are in place to support this growth.

Building a strong foundation is part of building a brand and developing that brand. Once you have created a brand, you need to live and breathe that brand in all you do and make sure it is growing every day. Building a brand and an identity will allow you to get better at all you do, and allow you to become known for success and great customer service.

Spending time on building a strong foundation and culture allows a large and successful business to be built and developed.

Understand what works and do more of it

Spend time understanding which parts of your business are working, which products sell the best, and which marketing strategies are the most successful - then do more of these. Any business that knows what works for them should implement more of those actions; it will grow and develop the business, and if it is currently successful, it will be making the customers happy.

The opposite side of this is to drop ideas and plans that do not work; this is often hard to implement. For example, you have spent a few months developing a new product range which turns out to sell very badly. You must drop the range and move on to developing another range that is better and more focused on the customers. Learn from the things that do not work, find out why they do not work and make sure you do not make the same mistakes again.

Focus on the things you are doing that work, that achieve your goals, and meet your strategic plans - do not do anything else, as it will not help you longer term and will not be making your customers happy.

Review all parts of your business:

- Analyse the information and data that exists in your business
- Ask the customers what is working and what is not working
- Find out from the team what is good and bad
- Develop the areas that work
- Drop the areas that do not work

Use new technologies

The world is ever-changing, with newer and faster technologies. Only a few years ago people mentioned the 'world wide web'; now we take it for granted, and most of us use it every day of our lives. The web has transformed business and will continue to develop in the future.

It is not just the internet that is changing business; new technologies are appearing every day and it is your role to find out what these are, how they can improve your business, and how they help to improve your customers' lives. These could be technical innovations that you can retail or new ways of developing products that means they are cheaper, more ethical or better.

An open mindset is needed as part of your culture; all ideas should be embraced and analysed to see if they could work in your business. Think outside the box and develop new and innovative solutions for your products and services – new ideas and inventions often seem crazy at the start, but over time they become the norm.

To find out about new technologies, innovations and inventions:

- Ask your customers what they are using now and what they want in the future
- Follow your industry news and see what is hot and new
- Watch your competition, have they worked out how to do things better, quicker, smarter?
- Embrace the internet and online shopping

- Develop and grow your use, and understanding, of social media - this is a massive new area of growth that can transform companies in the future

Grow with your customers

You have worked hard to gain your customers' trust and you must now keep them and develop with them. They will be growing in the world and experiencing new things, and you must find out what these are and what they want from your business.

Find out how they want to shop with you, interact with you and feel about your brand. Don't be afraid to test new ideas with them: new products, concepts or inventions. A loyal customer will feel valued if they are asked to attend a focus group reviewing your latest new product range or new gadget.

Understand how your customers are shopping and develop your offer to meet that growth. Whether that is social media, mobile commerce, kiosk shopping, etc., find out where they want to buy your products and how they want to buy them.

Ultimately, a good relationship with your customer can mean that they will invent your new product range for you. Remember, all you are trying to do is provide the customer with what they want, when they want it and at the price they are willing to pay - if you find out what they want for the future you can go and develop it for them.

Build and live your brand

Your brand and culture runs through everything you do, have done and will do, it is the unseen 'glue' that binds your business together. Making your brand strong, and 'living and breathing', is the key to a successful and sustainable future.

Summary

- Make your business's foundations strong
- Understand what works and do more of it
- Utilise new technologies
- Grow your business with your customers
- Build and 'live' your brand

Chapter 21

Etail And Social Media Case Study

The purpose of this case study is to talk you through the process we used to launch FreshMaxShirts.com and SmartWeave. The company was brand new to the market, with an exclusive new product. The challenge was that the company was unknown and had a breakthrough technology product, which people did not know existed or believed could work when they heard about it.

The journey started in 2009, eight years after the founders had started to develop a cotton fabric that did not show sweat patches – a high-quality fabric, made from 100% cotton, which felt like and acted like any high-quality premium cotton fabric. By 2009, the USA patent was granted and the rest of the world patents, including the UK and Europe, were pending. By this stage, hundreds of metres of fabric had been developed and tested; finally we had a fabric we could make into a men's shirt.

In late 2009 we set up a trading company whose purpose was to 'sell FreshMax Shirts online and commercially prove the technology and the fabric'.

The journey was challenging, and we had many pitfalls to conquer and decisions to make – I describe the main part of the journey now and the ultimate results for the business.

New brand, new name, new product

In 2009, we already had the name 'FreshMax', and we had
a blue and white logo designed a few years previously. This
logo was used solely in the discussions with other retailers,
while attempting to persuade them to sell our SmartWeave
fabric in their shirts.

We quickly realised that we needed a new brand, and in the
beginning we thought we wanted a new name and brand. The
previous image was 'sterile' and did not stand for anything – it
was literally the name written in blue and white. The imagery
and brand values were business- and technology-focused – we
needed a high-quality, customer-facing brand.

How we did it

We tested the idea of a new brand and new name with a
number of different agencies, and some even came up with
new names for the business, but we quickly realised that it

was best to stick to the original name and develop a new brand image and values for FreshMax.

Eventually, we employed a creative agency whose brief was to create a customer-facing brand for FreshMax and help explain the difference between the fabric business and the FreshMax brand as a shirt company.

The main goal was to keep the fabric brand separate from the shirts brand, so that we could sell the fabric to other retailers. The creative agency soon came up with 'FreshMaxShirts' for the shirts and 'SmartWeave' for the fabric.

During a two-week process, we talked about what we wanted from the brand and what our target market looked like. We had images and talked about what the customers' life was like, i.e. where they shopped, where they worked, their hobbies and the newspapers they read. From this, the creative team presented three possible images and logos for FreshMaxShirts and the one we use now immediately made the right impression with all three directors.

A logo was developed with the 'Max' part of the brand and an entire brand image started to develop. We also chose a number of real-life images of men in situations that we could see our customers in, to help define the final imagery and brand values.

Over the following few months we developed a set of brand guidelines that covered:

- Our brand – an introduction to the brand and what it was introducing to the world
- Before and after – what the world was like before the brand was developed and what the brand will bring to the world
- The brand proposition – an explanation of the product ranges and a brief outline of their USP
- The brand impact – the impact and level we were trying to achieve via the brand
- Our customers – the types of customers our brand targets and some information about them
- The brand statement – the words used to describe the brand to the outside world
- Tone of voice – how we should communicate with our customers and business partners
- Brand name usage – how and where we could use the brand name and in what formats
- Brand phrases – these are statements that help people understand the brand and what it stands for
- Brand values – the deep values and meanings of the brand

- Brand appearance – what the brand should look and appear like in all its differing uses
- Visual identity:
  - ⅄ The logo – the use of the logo in all its allowable formats
  - ⅄ The colour schemes and palettes
  - ⅄ Exclusion zones – where the logo should not be used
  - ⅄ Imagery – the photography and images that should be associated with the brand

All of this work was documented in the brand guidelines, which were then used to brief all the partners in our business. From the advertising agency to the shirt manufacturers, we made sure all the business partners understood the brand values and, more importantly, who our target customer was.

Set up and develop the website

Once we had developed a brand name and image, we needed to start the process of building a website from scratch. The website had to appeal to our target customers and had to encompass the latest developments in the online shopping experience.

Because of the start-up stage we were at, we also needed to rein in our ambitions and make sure the website was developed at the best value for the money we could afford, while setting up a brand and image that we wished to grow and develop.

The website had to address:

- Customer-facing needs:
  - ⚤ Have a one-page, easy-to-use checkout
  - ⚤ Compatible with all browsers and latest releases
  - ⚤ Be customer-friendly and easy to navigate
- 'Back-end' needs:
  - ⚤ Hold stock figures and manage the stock process
  - ⚤ Allow for offers and promotions
  - ⚤ Hold customers' details
  - ⚤ Upgradable for new technologies
  - ⚤ Allow an email database to be built and used regularly
  - ⚤ Integrated with the banks and secure online payment providers
  - ⚤ Ship to different countries
  - ⚤ Charge in different currencies
  - ⚤ Be simple for all the teams to operate and use

How we did it

We found a partner agency who worked with us to design the 'wire frame'. A wire frame is a description of all the website pages, all the functionality and a diagram depicting the main areas and imagery on the website.

Once this was developed, the creative agency and the web partner worked together on the final designs and imagery.

Many emails and meetings later, we had a website that was customer-facing and met the requirements for our brand and image.

The website was changed over the first few weeks, but started life like the picture above.

The back end of the website was built, and the system was integrated into the payment system and the bank accounts. Stock was loaded on to the system, and we had our first range of shirts arriving from Morocco to be photographed for the website.

It was all a big rush in the end, and we were still working on the website the night before the launch date – even though we had planned this for more than six months.

Develop a supply chain

In late 2009, we had a manufacturing partner in France that we knew could make the fabric for the shirts (this took two years of development for them to perfect the fabric manufacturing process), but we did not have a shirt manufacturer, and at that stage we had only ever made a few test shirts. We had to start work on the supply chain alongside the development of the brand and the website.

We engaged with the French team and soon narrowed down Romania and Morocco as the best places to manufacture good quality men's shirts. We arranged a visit to four Moroccan factories and four Romanian factories in early 2010. Following these visits, we asked four factories for a full sample and a full costing - the shirts must be manufactured in a certain way and must use certain processes, and we needed to test whether the suppliers could make the shirts to our high specifications.

The process was very challenging; we had less than six months to make a full range of brand new shirts, using a brand new supply chain and fabric. The French team took full control of the sourcing and supply chain and helped us agree with a Moroccan partner for the first range and first order for delivery to our customers.

We now had a partner, but no shirt design or cut. In spring 2010 we went to Morocco with a number of shirts and in two days we developed and designed the new FreshMax Shirt fit and style. This was difficult because we knew we were selling the shirts in the UK and Europe and needed a 'European' fit.

We now had the style of the shirt and left the French team managing the manufacture and finishing of the fabric needed for launch, and the process to book and manufacture the shirts in Morocco.

The sourcing strategy we had planned and agreed meant that we would also use the French partners for the warehousing and dispatch.

Pricing and promotional strategy

We kept the promotional and pricing strategy very simple from day one; we wanted a premium shirt available to the middle market. This reflected the uniqueness of the shirt and the quality of the fabric and manufacturer.

We researched the target customer to understand the types of shirts they wore and the types of shops they visited to purchase their shirts.

How we did it

We identified our competitors and reviewed their pricing strategies. We knew we had a unique benefit, so we priced high so that we could compete with a 20%-off promotion. All our shirts are the same price in the UK and we set differential pricing in Europe, USA and Rest of the World.

The pricing policy was to remain simple and offer a promotional offer for the important periods and for new launches, etc.

All our financial models and projections were based on a 20%-off retail price. We used the 20% for the launch and special periods and for the rest of the periods we used partner and affiliate offers to help drive sales and raise awareness.

Develop a marketing strategy

This was a major challenge and we had two main problems here:

1. Nobody had ever heard of a shirt that does not show sweat patches

2. Sweat is a negative issue that we needed to talk about without offending our customers

How we did it

The creative partners were also part of the marketing team and led the marketing planning for us. We spent a few days discussing what we should say about the shirt, breaking the functions of the shirt down into benefits for our target customer segment.

We defined our target market as: a shirt wearer in the South East, aged 25-50 years, works in an office and wants to look his best all the time.

We had to segment the market, in order to start a marketing campaign and be able to sell to our first customers. In theory, the shirt should be available for every man and woman in the world, but we needed to target a very defined market in the beginning.

From this segment, we defined it further and focused our entire launch campaign on the London office workers in Canary Wharf. We realised that there are more than a million men in that area each day - concentrating on launching the business in such an area would be the most efficient and effective plan.

The message and brand strapline took a few weeks to develop. We had to be careful about mentioning 'sweat' as it is a personal and emotional word, but the benefit of our shirts was that you did not show sweat patches and therefore the shirt was great for all men - and we needed to tell them this.

The discussion always led us to the benefits being 'improved confidence'; if you have sweat patches you notice it and you are aware of it. This makes you less comfortable and in turn less confident. A scientific study also showed us that once you are aware of sweating you sweat more - we knew we had to talk about how the product made the customer feel 'confident and free'.

We eventually decided on the strapline: 'Show nothing but confidence'. This encapsulated all we wanted to say about the benefits of the shirt; it was our strapline at launch and still is to this day.

We also developed a sentence that described the shirts - we had to say what they were so that the customers could understand the product.

We used: 'The only shirt that eliminates sweat patches'.

This strong sentence was important to explain what a FreshMax Shirt was and why you should buy it - it describes our USP.

The next stage was to develop the adverts; these had to centre on sweat, but not the negative images of sweat – we needed 'confident and free' images and statements.

We used two of our brand images of the customers and made two separate adverts based on improving your confidence:

1. Meeting the Board? No Sweat – a confident man with his arms back looking like he is the most confident person in the board room.

2. First date nerves? No Sweat – a very happy young man with his arm around a beautiful girl, looking and feeling very content without any sweat patches.

The adverts had a theme that highlighted an occasion when you would feel nervous and start to sweat more than normal, and ended with 'No Sweat', as this was what the shirt guaranteed the customer. A great benefit of 'No Sweat' was that its second meaning is to relax and take it easy – this was exactly how our customers wanted to feel in a stressful situation.

The adverts were now agreed, and we set up the Marketing and Advertising campaign. This was very simple: focus on Canary Wharf and London commuters.

We launched in July 2010 with paid-for advertising:

- *City AM* (London City based free newspaper)
- *The Metro* (the free London commuter paper – mainly given out at tube stations where it is very hot and sweaty in the summer)
- A two-week poster campaign in Canary Wharf (With the 'Board Meeting? No Sweat' tagline as we were targeting the office workers in the Canary Wharf complex)
- A massive PR campaign

Launch and PR

Launching and PR for our product was the most important area to get right, as we were a new technology product retailer, and also the area where we were likely to get the most success if we got it right. We had to develop a PR programme that would launch a totally new brand and totally new technological product to the whole world, but focusing on the target customer in UK and London.

How we did it

We found a great PR partner, who had previous experience in launching new products to the market, and also knew the press and TV contacts we needed for our product. We worked with the PR partner, advertising partner and creative partner to agree a plan to launch the product in July 2010.

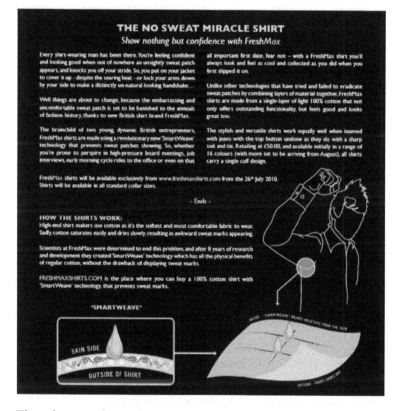

The plan was based on two stories:

1. The product technology itself and what the benefits of the world's first shirt to eliminate sweat patches would be

2. The development story of two young English guys
who spent eight years developing the technology

The plan was set up to send the PR introduction sheets to the press, magazines, TV, bloggers, etc. and then follow up with meetings and product samples.

The PR campaign was a massive success, and on the day of launch the inventors appeared on ITV1 with an interview and a full two-minute test of the product. In the video, the ITV presenter wore the shirt on a bike and in a sauna, proving the technology worked. This was the perfect start to the business launch and helped prove that the shirts really do exist and they do stop sweat patches showing – even in a sauna.

That was followed by the BBC Sunday morning show, *Something for the Weekend*, where the product was discussed and tested again. The press and magazines coverage then took hold of the story, and we were in most of the main newspapers and magazines during the first six months of launch.

A massive turning point for the business was a Reuters TV interview with the inventors. Filmed over a couple of days, this turned into a Reuters video that was sent out to more than 200 countries. It was immediately picked up on news channels in the Czech Republic and Sweden. Subsequently, it was found in the news in Indonesia and India.

By January 2011, we had PR coverage in all national UK newspapers, the BBC and ITV1, Reuters news networks, a large number of magazines and international coverage, including a Sunday newspaper in Australia and a fashion magazine in the USA.

The physical launch was followed up by a massive online campaign. Using social networks (Facebook, Twitter and YouTube) we set up a two-month campaign, which made sure the news was sent out on a regular basis – mainly links to the TV and newspaper articles.

We also commissioned a video to be filmed, and set up to become a 'viral' campaign on the internet, to create a fun image with our shirts.

We filmed a Boris Johnson (the Mayor of London) look-alike, wearing our shirts and riding a TFL bike. We used a stunt bike rider to perform stunts and sent the video to many blogging sites, which in turn used the social media channels to 'viral' the video.

Customer service and fulfilment

Customer service was key to providing a high-quality service that matched the image and the brand values. This had to be done to a high standard, but also be based on a start-up budget.

The fulfilment, warehousing and dispatch were to be handled by our French partners, who would take the orders off the system twice a day and dispatch directly from France.

The customer service was to be via email and a call centre to handle the queries and reply to customers within a reasonable timescale.

How we did it

From the start of the planning, we set up an area in the French warehouse to manage the FreshMax Shirts stock and dispatch process. A system was developed to print labels and invoices, to ensure we could pick and pack the shirts for each customer and send them ASAP.

We negotiated a contract with the French postal service that meant the costs were reasonable, and we could track all our deliveries to our customers. If we needed to send the shirts fast we used a courier.

The call centre was outsourced. The agents were trained and given access to the systems to track orders and answer basic queries. Any difficult queries were escalated to the FreshMax UK team for answering.

An email template system was set up to answer basic customer queries in a quick and efficient process. The FAQs section of the website covered the most basic questions and was updated as new common questions were asked by customers.

Returns were handled by the FreshMax UK team and managed via communications with the French warehouse team, making sure they were handled quickly and efficiently.

The results

The FreshMaxShirts.com journey was nine months from initial idea to launch day – this **was very fast**, and involved many people and a massive investment in time and resources.

The launch was a major success with the TV and press PR, backed up by advertising in London, which meant a good beginning for the new technology product and the ecommerce website.

Licensing the technology

Once the fabric and technology was commercially proven, the business was then able to grow the licensing part of the business, under the brand name of FreshMax Shirts in a number of countries. In these countries, expert retailers bought the finished shirts and sold them via their own networks using their local knowledge of the retail markets.

This is an excellent way to grow a retail business in countries where you do not have the local expertise and do not know how the customers in that market will respond to your products.

This was then followed by own-brand licensing and fabric deals, the first of which was with Marks and Spencer PLC. Since April 2011, the shirts have been available in Marks and Spencer PLC, using the technology of FreshMax Shirts and branded as 'Dry Extreme Shirts' by Marks and Spencer.

It is interesting to see that M&S used a similar branding to the original FreshMax logo – it shows the differentiation of their business and their target market versus those of the FreshMax Shirts brand.

The shirts can now be seen in a number of retailers across the world and are still available at FreshMaxShirts.com.

Highlights of the success

- Successful launch of FreshMax Shirts as a brand and launch of SmartWeave as the fabric technology was achieved in only nine months
- Sales in over 24 countries across the world, including Australia and the USA
- TV coverage across the world
- Press coverage across the world
- Social media coverage in many countries and many different languages
- Successful advertising campaign in London and many people still recall the adverts from the Metro
- New products in the pipeline (including linen, women's and trousers)
- Global sales of the fabric direct to retailers

Acknowledgements

For all my friends and family (V, A, B, C, K and M).

I mostly want to thank my gran, who has helped me shape the history part of the book. It was her father who started our retail world back in 1923.

Over the last five years, I have been to spend time with her in Canada, where she emigrated at 70 years of age! Her memories and stories have helped bring to life the history of retailing and I am pleased to be able to share that detail in this book.

Thanks to Gran and Jack for starting our retail world.

About The Author

Antony specialises in retail and ecommerce and has more than twenty years of experience in the retail industry, including fifteen years learning from the large retailers (Marks & Spencer, Sainsbury's, Dixons Retail). He also has experience working with smaller retailers, including the set up, and subsequent sale, of a successful online retailer.

Born into a retailing family and starting work in a newsagent at the age of 15, Antony fell in love with retail and this passion has progressed throughout his life.

When he was at college he started work at Sainsbury's and soon progressed to the customer service team. With retail firmly in his blood he went to Loughborough University to study retail management for four years, including a year working in Mark & Spencer stores. This is where he started to learn the real detail of running a successful retail business. After Antony graduated, he moved to London to join the

Sainsbury's graduate programme and spent two years working in Sainsbury's headquarters in trading and property roles.

He then returned to Marks and Spencer, where he spent five years working in HQ, learning the trade in areas such as store development, buying and merchandising.

He spent the following five years at Dixons Retail, where he looked after the UK ecommerce sites, the Dixons chain, a B2B company and spent two years in the Czech Republic creating a new European Shared Service Centre (finalist in the European Shared Service awards). His last role was Commercial Finance Director for the UK.

Antony set up the retail arm of SmartWeaveShirts.com – the world's only fabric which eliminates sweat patches – taking the business from a shirt fabric to a global shirt technology company selling in 26 countries. He has since launched four ecommerce websites for fashion brands and a TV shopping company.

Antony uses his vast retail and ecommerce experience to advise and develop global retailers and brands online and has worked with HP, Boots, Reckitt Benkiser, B&Q, Benefit Cosmetics and Deckers brands, to name but a few.

Please contact us for further information about our services and for free downloads at: www.retailpotential.com

Join in the conversation @AntonyWelfare